ON INDIAN HISTORY

ON INDIAN HISTORY

A STUDY IN METHOD

DHURJATI PRASAD MUKERJI

GYAN

Published by

GYAN

Gyan Publishing House
5, Ansari Road
Daryaganj, New Delhi-110002
Phone: 011-47034999, 9811692060
E-mail: books@gyanbooks.com

Distribution Network
gyanbooks.com
India, USA, Canada, UK, Australia

ISBN: 978-93-7169-639-5 (PB)

First Published, 1945

2nd Impression 2025

Printed at: Gyan Press, Delhi.

ON INDIAN HISTORY
Author: DHURJATI PRASAD MUKERJI

ON INDIAN HISTORY

A STUDY IN METHOD

BY

DHURJATI PRASAD MUKERJI

UNIVERSITY OF LUCKNOW

HIND KITABS

PUBLISHERS : BOMBAY

TO

THE FAMILY TREE

IN

HISTORICAL GRATITUDE

PREFACE

These pages are mainly addressed to those who feel that Indian History has to be rewritten. The dissatisfaction with the available textbooks, in spite of their scholarship, is deep and wide-spread. But there is little examination and less clarification of the fundamentals involved. Now that at least two stupendous ventures on the subject have been launched under the best of auspices, it is expected that the errors of the past will be rectified and that a genuine understanding of the processes which have made India what she is, will be possible. That hope is the emotional background of this book.

The author feels that the first defect of our historical scholarship has been the result of a misunderstanding of the methodology of History. While it is imperative that the scientific method should be strictly observed, its limitations, particularly in regard to its applicability to the changing human, socio-historical materials and processes, as also its logical development, should at the same time be duly considered. This is likely to yield a few tendencies and generalizations whose active co-operation is essential for rewriting the history of India, an object desired by all Indians. To have a host of eminent Indian historians and to build up a science of History are noble desires by themselves, but the desires must serve India's future history. There is not much sense in adding one more discipline to the list of sciences of contemplation in which India has specialized unless that discipline leads to positive, socio-historical action. Thus it is that an enquiry into the methodology of History becomes the intellectual compulsion of these pages. The author has an idea that the Marxist approach may be found suitable in the circumstances.

It would have been better if this task were performed by more competent men. The author is not a 'professional' historian, but a layman who retains connexions with his old interests. The allegiance of three generations is also hard to overcome. When this personal weakness is fortified by the conviction that Indian History is essentially social, then a sociologist's intrusion should be pardonable.

The author is grateful to the Editor of *Social Welfare* for his kind permission to expand some of the articles published there. Two chapters are based upon talks given at the A.I.R., Lucknow, for which thanks are due to the authorities. The necessary adaptation has been made in the interest of the unity of the subject. But for the ungrudging assistance of my student, Mr Harish Chandra, the publication of the volume would have been impossible. Dr G. N. Dhaon, a colleague of mine in the Politics Department, very kindly read the typescript and offered valuable suggestions.

The author hopes that the spirit running through these pages will be appreciated—at least, not be misunderstood, by our historians.

Feb. 1945. D. P. Mukerji

CONTENTS

INTRODUCTION

It is highly regrettable that the various textbooks of Indian History and the numerous special works on its particular periods, excellent though they be of their kind, have but seldom exposed to the readers in general and the Youth of India in particular the fundamental forces which in the plenitude of their functioning had accounted for the greatness of Indian life and culture in certain epochs and which in their state of slump, depression and low vigilance had made for quiescence, subjection and misery. Indian History, as it has been written, is a story either of high lights or of dull tones. And yet Indian culture, more than any other complex pattern, has persisted and preserved many of its pristine features. This fact of continued uniqueness or specificity awaits explanation not in terms of an impressionistic or intuitive apprehension of the Divine Will or of Destiny and Genius, but in those of causal sequence. What, however, has been attempted so far in that line is tautological. The caste-system, the more or less autonomous geographical unit, the comparative security that India has enjoyed from external aggression, the continued existence of an elite-group, viz. the Brahmins, are at best paraphrases of the fact of persistence. They do not really explain why the spine of the caste-system still holds erect, how the hosts of aggressors have been assimilated to evolve the form of Indian culture as it is today, and why the elite-group is still in possession of social prestige. Surely, there must be some general laws, some purpose, some meaning governing and attached to these phenomena that arise from the continuity of Indian History. An honest reader may knock his head at the feet of India's historians and still fail to receive a satisfactory explanation of such problems.

To my mind the sources of this deficiency are two: the absence of sociological approach ; and the absence of any philosophy of History. My argument stands on the following propositions : (a) Indian History is more than political history, because the Austinian view of the State and the government never displaced the organistic-cum-religious, that is to say, the cultural view of an all-comprehending society ; (b) Indian History is more than mere economic history, because in India the feudal-primitive modes and relations of production have ruled the longest with their adequate ideologies often acting, for that very reason, as it were on their own. Indian History is thus essentially the histories of pre-industrial societies, cultures, and nationalities federated or confederated into a union. If the above be true, the avoidance of sociology and philosophy in the understanding of Indian historical events is doubly regrettable. The two sources of deficiency can, however, be reduced to one if we equate, following the master-minds of the nineteenth century, Philosophy of History with Sociology. Modern thinkers in other contexts have sought to separate them ; but considering that the application of a method is relative to the age and that the need of a new conception of History in the India of the twentieth century is more or less similar to that of Europe after the French Revolution, we Indians can for the present remain content with the older identification so long as we avoid the mistakes of the historical and the social thought of the nineteenth century Europe, viz. the importation of theology in one form or another into the explanation of human events or, in reaction, the reduction of human materials to mechanical entities. The supreme need of historical scholarship in India is therefore a philosophy of History, with proper safeguards against theology and mechanics.

We will not raise the question whether History can have a philosophy or not. The views of those who hold that History and Philosophy are two distinct disciplines living like porcupines in fear of each other are well known. So are those of scholars who without the necessary knowledge of the methodology of sciences proclaim that History is of the order of a natural science and therefore cannot have any philosophy. All that we need say at this stage of our enquiry is that 'anybody who has a philosophy, that is, a consciously thought out standpoint of opinion, must have a philosophy of History . . . Our philosophy of History is part of our politics : the object of knowledge when assimilated becomes part of our active will.' (A. Coates : *A Pluralistic View of History*—Journal of Philosophy, Vol. VIII, p. 318.) In other words, the chief fallacy in the position of the so-called 'scientific' historians is revealed if we pose it in a statement that involves not the status of any abstract body of knowledge called History but the function of any human being who participates in the historical process and inherits it in the form of traditions and whose view of history is part of and whose conscious action adds to and re-creates that process itself. History is not the special preserve of 'scientific' historians ; it is the bread and salt of every single person with active will. 'Scientific' History is an account of castrated wills.

And then push home the arguments of these 'scientifics' and 'positivists', and you find that their 'science' fails at the ultimate stage. In almost every case, be it an attempt at the reduction of History to Biology or Physiology, Physical Geography or Psychology, even to Energetics, the real content of History, viz. the flux of social life as it is lived and changed by human beings, is barred out of the sphere of investigation and traced to some *inner* law which by this sleight of hand automatically becomes the explanation. If, on the contrary, the search for any generalization is renounced in the name of factual research, a clear-cut division of labour between historians and philosophers is smoothly effected. But such a division shares the defect of the Smithian division of labour. No division of labour is a full separation; every division emphasizes the social complexity and interdependence. As the famous Russian historian A. I. Tiumeniev writes in criticism of Windelband and Rickert: 'The consequence of this division of labour between the historians and the philosophers was the complete subjection of history to philosophy and the transformation of historical science into the serving maid of idealist philosophy and at the same time the resurrection of the philosophy of history in the old metaphysical and theological sense of the word. With the aim of making better use of history in this direction it is separated from the other sciences as being a specially "individualizing" science; a science of non-repetitive facts, a science in which actions according to an aim and teleology take the place of causality, a science, therefore, in which all law is denied.' Thus it is that the scientific search for laws defeats itself by the initial premise of a separation between philosophy and history—a separation which really ensues from disregarding man as the central theme of the historical process. Be it noted that the fault does not lie either with philosophy or with history ; it is in having a particular philosophy, viz. the idealistic, and in having a particular view of historical science, viz. the mechanistic.

The errors which beset the path of the idealist philosopher of History are familiar to students of Hegel. Those which make Croce stumble are less familiar. As Hegel after envisaging the grand stages of historical evolution in search of the Absolute came home to the Prussian State and to his own Self (read Heine), so has Croce after traversing the tortuous path of Hegelianism and Marxism returned to Spirit and Freedom to formulate his own brand of historiography. For Croce, economics, the domain of private utility, is distinct from ethics, aesthetics, science and history, and as such can 'grow from its own roots as a flourishing and (almost) independent spiritual body.' Such a view dissevers the human being into unreal components. Its logical premise is that the Spirit is 'a unity of distincts, not a tension of opposites' leading up to a synthesis. Croce denies the possibility of Universal Philosophy on the same ground as he denies the possibility of Universal History, viz., that the Spirit moves as it wills, although he would define History as the Story of Liberty. He really equates Philosophy with History because he thinks that both are manifestations of the self-consciousness of Life itself, its processes and evolutions. Says he : 'When chronicle has been reduced to its proper practical and mnemonical function, and history has been raised to the knowledge of the eternal present, it shows itself to be identical with philosophy, which for its part is never anything but the thought of the eternal present.' (Quoted in John Laird's *Recent Philosophy*, p. 62.) It is in this special sense that Croce's famous remark that all History is contemporary History is to be understood. That is to say, as Laird points out, for Croce, History is a stir, a 'vibration of life' in 'the reflective spirit'. There would not be much harm in it if the life of reflection were not so distinct, as it is with Croce, from the life of the practical. One could, following Laird again, also raise a vulgar query as to the difference between the passing mood and the eternal present, as to how a historian can sum up in his present thought the past with any sense unless the past were a real past and the present a real present. Again, unless the past be real, contemporaneity will have to exclude any surviving influence. Is not the contemporary view of history also an integral part of the historical process itself? The real defect of Croce's approach, in fact of any idealistic philosophy of history, is that thought or knowledge or reflection with its general, scientific and abstract laws is not integrated with existence which is concrete, personal and social; and History must needs work on both levels at one and the same time. Burckhardt in his *Reflections on History* betrays the same disintegration although, unlike Croce, he disowns any open alliance with Philosophy.* For such idealistic and pseudo-idealistic historians, History means a number of things to be shifted according to convenience.

The idealist philosophers of history are not the only culprits in this matter of ambiguity. There is a certain school of materialist historians, for example those whom Lenin called the 'Economists', who use the word 'economy' in at least three different signifi-

**Vide* Ch. 8.

cances and move from the one to the other without compunction. In their hand the economic factor may mean (a) the biological needs, (b) the technological equipments or the state of science, and (c) the material, i.e. the natural resources and their exploitation. Now it would not be very wrong if each meaning were stuck to throughout the analysis and discourse. What actually happens is that between the premise and the conclusion the three meanings are telescoped. Even that would be permissible provided Economics were a branch of poetry or written in Joycean prose. Scientific analysis, however, requires plain. categorical statements of propositions. The situation is further complicated by the fact that while the biological needs are stable, the technological factors are less so, that while the material resources are more or less constant, their exploitation is unequal and elastic. In other words, each factor has its own tempo of change or exploitation. Naturally, the 'Economist's' super-structure of ideas can hardly be anything more than a haze or a mist, although he calls it a reflection. Logically too, if the reflection were precise or exact, historical explanation becomes tautological: historical change becomes equivalent to *all* changes. In reality, however, history often halts and forgets; it suffers from paralysis and aphasia. This mistake arising from Economism. viz. the isolation and the disintegration of the economic function, is not committed by the Marxist historian.*

Therefore, the task of the Indian historian is clear. He must have a philosophy of history; he cannot afford to have an idealist philosophy of his-

Vide Ch. I.

tory; he must needs cling to science to secure reliable evidence and to the inductive temper for interpretation; but he cannot be a mechanical scientist. At the same time, being primarily interested in changing and making history for the purpose of living better and still better he cannot develop the neutrality of the so-called scientific attitude. As Woodbridge has so aptly put it in *The Purpose of History* (p. 89): *History is, then, not only the conserving, the remembering, and the understanding of what has happened: it is also the completing of what has happened. And since in man history is consciously lived, the completing of what has happened is also the attempt to carry it to what he calls perfection. He looks at a wilderness, but even as he looks, beholds a garden. For him, consequently, the purpose of history is not a secret he vainly tries to find, but a kind of life his reason enables him to live. As he lives it well the fragments of existence are completed and illumined in the visions they reveal.*

Does the Indian historian look at a wilderness and behold a garden? Does he divulge a kind of life which his reason enables him to live, to live well, to live better and to live whole? If he does not, his philosophy is at fault and not his research. The future historian of India must do it all, for the Indian life as it is lived today is a wilderness, fragmented and irrational. For him the supreme question is whether to treat history as a noun or as a verb. In short, with the help of his materials and methods and by virtue of his being an Indian living in this century, the Indian historian must re-make the history of India. And this is the charge the following pages seek to bear, inadequately but, I hope, sincerely.

1. INDIAN HISTORY AND THE MARXIST METHOD

I

The History of Civilisation edited by C. K. Ogden is probably the most authoritative series on the subject in the English language. It is an extension of the French venture, *L' Evolution de L' Humanite*, which was being edited by the French historian M. Henri Berr before the War. None but the ripest of scholars have written for these two series. To the English series only two Indian scholars were asked to contribute—Professor N. K. Sidhanta, on the Heroic Age of India, and Professor G. S. Ghurye, on Caste and Race in India. These two volumes are classics of their kind. Since then, three professers of the European continent, Paul Masson-Oursel, Philippe Stern, both of Paris, and Helena De William-Grabowska of the University of Cracow have collaborated to produce a volume in French on Ancient India and Indian Civilization. It has been translated into English and forms the only treatise in the two series on Indian Civilization as a whole. Brilliantly written, it has become popular in academic circles. The French Editor's Foreword is an essay on the Indian Genius. Strange comments have been made there. Here are a few samples which we bring to the notice of that large number of Indians who are looking forward to the projected ventures on Indian History with some excitement but without much definiteness in their expectations.

'History can be events, or the memory of events. The Indians have lacked the memory of events, or rather they have lacked not writing, but the use of writing, to record them.' 'India has never been interested in facts.' 'They (Indians) turn to it (the past) for lessons and claims to glory. The truth does not concern them.' 'It has no history, first, in the sense that its past does not offer clearly distinct phases such as our own antiquity and Middle Ages, or the periods before and after Christ. From the Aryan invasion to the coming of Islam, India is extraordinarily continuous in time. In space, on the other hand, it is extraordinarily discontinuous.' Thus far M. Berr. Be it said on his behalf that these remarks are the conclusions he draws from the accounts in the volume itself. When M. Masson-Oursel writes that the very mind of the Indians 'seems to have a distaste for history,' or when Mme. William-Grabowska declares that 'every opposition was made to the spread of knowledge to the lower classes,' we can understand the source of the editorial comments.

Let us first make our position clear. For us and our like the days of Swadeshi agitation are over. In that genuinely romantic period, we had invested one legacy of Western Liberalism, viz. Nationalism, and received high dividends in the shape of pride in our ancient history. In other words, our sense of history was the product of a renaissance under the impact of the West, both as action and reaction. Sanskrit learning, the use of Persian. socio-religious unity, had all but disappeared ; in its place was reared an impersonal, all-Indian, administrative unity which was fortified by the spread of communications and the popularity of foreign ideas among the new elite. We had to discover a counterpart for all that for our self-respect. But today. we no longer seek to fill the present with the golden deeds of the past. Nor do we find it a profitable occupation to compensate our political subjection with the help of ancient glory. Our present attitude is positive and objective. The scientific spirit has so seeped into the bases of our scholarship that any imaginative structure which we might raise shakes and falls into dust at the blast of facts. We are not vain ; we may even be sorry at some turns of events, excluding of course, the British conquest which, besides forging a 'providential' connexion, has given us the 'sense' and the 'facts' of history. At the same time we do not feel ashamed. That would be unscientific. A palaeontologist is not ashamed of fossils, a zoologist is not ashamed of the origins of life and the gaps in its evolution, a doctor is not ashamed of glands and bacteria. No scientist is ever apologetic of his data. His shame and sorrow lie in his ignorance of facts caused by his own indifference, the inadequacy of his premises, the weakness of his logic and the incapacity of his judgement. Thanks to the scientific spirit, if we have ceased to be chauvinists, we have also ceased to be ashamed of our past. *Our attitude is one of humility towards the given fund. But it is also an awareness of the need, the utter need, of recreating the given and making it a flow. The given of India is very much in ourselves. And we want to make something worthwhile out of it, and at this crisis of India and the world.* The new ventures on Indian History stand or fall by the success of this attempt. No account of Indian History can endure if it does not recognize facts and events, but it must be instinct with that sense which goes beyond a display of data. That sense none of the authors quoted at the beginning possesses. And yet their approach is 'scientific'. Something is wrong there. We do not seriously mind the pejorative remarks, because we feel that India can survive her 'history'. In this essay we are concerned with *the Method of History* itself in order that a satisfactory History of India may be available to Indians.

By all means let us have science and scholarship. But is scholarship enough? A scientific attitude is essential. But does it exhaust the 'logical' approach? Caution towards accredited facts is one of the precious qualities of human intellect, but human intellect has other possibilities too, some of which are bold enough to use the quantity of recorded and accurate facts for wider purposes, such as reconstructing history. Are we so sure that the old methods of natural sciences are applicable to the social and the historical? Some of the best methodologists of Science and of History think that they are not. Jevons in his *Principles of Science* (p. 761) said that the Science of History in the true sense of the term was 'an absurd notion'. Dilthey, probably the greatest of modern historical methodologists, whose one great conviction was that History alone could show what Humanity was, gave the assurance that the humanistic sciences had an autonomy of their own. 'Their material is the special sciences, their principle the autonomy, that is, the freedom of thinking and of human life itself.' He is anti-metaphysical, sceptical, analytical, descriptive in facts, 'scientific' enough to satisfy all tests. But all his stupendous learning is directed towards making 'culture declare itself' by the pressure of 'understanding'. Such an 'understanding' is not mere intellection; it is 'cumulative, massive and brooding', it is a new way of grasping the total reality without fragmenting it into simpler parts as 'scientific' explanations succeed in doing. Dilthey's great contribution to the methodology of humanistic studies consists in extending this 'understanding' to include historical experience and expression. The tension between the concept of a people's *Weltanschauung* and its scientific proof, which had worked to the detriment both of philosophy and history, Dilthey wants to relieve by substituting a critique of Historical Reason for that of Pure Reason. Leaving aside the importance of such a view for the subsequent course of Philosophy we may conclude that since Dilthey it should be difficult for any significant historian to ignore the first premise of the writing of history, viz. that History, its approach, its attitude, its method—are bound up with historical experience, with 'historical human life, originating from it, and reacting upon it'. Naturally, as historical experience differs from epoch to epoch and from country to country, 'understanding' and expression cannot be of a uniform pattern which the procedure of natural sciences would impose or occasion.

Another great historian of our time has been Troeltsch. He too declared that History has its own methods to 'coax historical matter of fact in its wholeness to declare its fundamental trend'. He pleaded for the unique with the special inquirers, and for the singular with those who, like M. Berr, would equate 'true history with the history of mankind' and make of it a 'chaos of ostensible world-totalities'. His concept of 'Kultur', each with its own concrete and individual wholeness, is one grand protest against the abstractness of general laws popularized by the mechanical sciences and their application to the sphere of the relative. Troeltsch's method is exemplified in his monumental works on Christian Thought, *Social Teaching of the Christian*

Churches and *Ideas of Natural Laws and Humanity*. In fact, for the first time, the Sociology of Culture seems to have carved its own niche in the temple of Clio. While admitting the great value of such a method and its attraction for an Indian historian—conscious as he cannot but be of the definiteness of India's '*Kultur*' with its own '*Sinn und Wesen*' dominated by religious and spiritual traditions which mark it off from the definiteness of, say, the Western European Culture—it is difficult to uphold with Troeltsch that the concreteness of the individual whole is only to be 'intuitively' grasped. Intuition has its own important place in every sphere of life. It is a short cut to understanding and action ; it occasionally seizes parts and aspects of reality denied to intellect ; it fosters what has been called 'empathy', i.e. a sympathetic penetration and an immanence amounting to identity ; it is often very real. At the same time, it is likely to be highly selective, and neglectful of other aspects and implications. It carries no guarantee of self-correction and tends to feel superior to rectification by other sources. Being proud of its efficiency it separates itself from the patient processes of logic which have built up the scientific method. All these merits and demerits of intuitive approach are present in Troeltsch's writings. His logic of historical understanding is distinct from the logic by which the very substance of History, viz. human experience, is guided. As Professor Morris Ginsberg puts it in his paper on History and Sociology read at the Anglo-American Conference of Historians, 1931 (*Studies in Sociology*): 'There can be no doubt that he (Troeltsch) is right in insisting that history must of necessity start with concrete entities and not with supposed primary atomic elements. There can also be no doubt of the value of the notion of individual wholes which to my mind, as actually used by historians, are extremely complex concepts summing up the historian's vision of the concrete life of a period or of a group of events. But it may be doubted whether the cognitive processes by which such concepts are constructed really differ in kind from those which are involved in the work of the natural sciences. There is in any event no magical potency in such concepts as the Renaissance, and their explanatory value depends upon the extent to which they embody detailed and painstaking analysis of the forces involved and the possibility of their being ultimately related to the fundamental laws of life and mind . . . In the absence of such detailed analytic studies the concept of individual wholes . . . may lead to interesting subjective impressions, but hardly to a rational understanding of the phenomena of history.' Above all, even that empathetic understanding which is rendered possible by the interpretation of an individual whole in terms of the values of the whole leads inevitably to historical relativism which makes it difficult to understand the continuous growing of values. (Mandelbaum : *The Problem of Historical Knowledge*, Chs. 2, 4 and 9.) The danger of intuitive approach is great in the case of Indian history. By it, all Indian History is reducible to the history of Hinduism or Buddhism, to the history of Islam or of the British conquest. That conclusion, however, runs counter to the persistence of the processes of Indian living up to the present day ; it extinguishes all possibilities of further growth in the light of today's problems ; it limits all Indian History to the history of concepts and ideas which obviously are more easily seizable by intuition than the actual conditions of living on the material plane. We do not suggest that Troeltsch was oblivious of the economic substructure. He also shares with Max Weber the honour of being the founder of Culture-Sociology. We further note his emphasis on action as against historical contemplation'. But his 'intuitionalism' cannot be accepted as the method of History.

So, on the strength of Dilthey's and Troeltsch's arguments, we come to the conclusion that the eminent authors and the editor of the volume on Ancient India and Indian Civilization whom we have quoted at the beginning of this essay grievously erred on the score of methodology. Their understanding was vitiated by the attempt to read Indian history as a part of European history, i.e. by an inability to appreciate India even as an individual whole in terms of her own values, or what comes to the same thing, by an eagerness to think of History as Unity with laws, materials and procedure common to all countries and epochs. Such an approach, however, is nothing special to these Continental scholars; in fact, it is shared by the upholders of the Trotskyan view of History as adumbrated in his theory of World Revolution, by a number of English historians of India no less than by Indian historians themselves who in the name of 'scientific method' miss the specific features of India's history. For them and their like Dilthey and Troeltsch should prove the best antidote. And yet, an antidote is often a dangerous prescription. Dilthey's 'understanding' and Troeltsch's 'intuition' may easily mean a severance from logical analysis and painstaking research. It may end by making Indian history into a mystery. Besides, no intuitive understanding of the individual whole called India can change the face of India towards the desired goal, viz. democratic freedom, in any real sense of the two terms. For aught we know, such 'intuitive understanding' by German historians of German history and German genius may have been largely responsible for the ideology of Nazism (De Rohan Butler : *The Roots of National Socialism*). India can ill afford that luxury. Therefore, we want a method which would respect the special features making up the Indian pattern without cutting adrift from the sheet-anchor of historical analysis ; in other words, we demand a method which would pay due regard to the relativity of Indian history and yet put it in the perspective of the evolving world-history. This method would not be afraid of demarcating the subject-matter of History from that of the Natural Sciences where the difference exists, and would comprehend the rest of the field where Nature and Man meet. It would finally be more than a mere intellectual exercise. It would show us Indians the way to make our History. Such a method is offered by Marxism.

II

Karl Marx's place as a historian is of the highest order. Edmund Wilson (a non-Marxist), in that most penetrating book on the art and science of History as practised by the masters from Vico, Michelet down to Lenin, *To the Finland Station*, thinks that Marx's writings on French history and politics are supreme achievements of their kind. It is also well-known how Karl Marx called his system 'scientific' in opposition to the Utopian schemes of preceding socialists. There are some honest thinkers who hold that 'his sociology is the genuine social science of our time.' We do not propose to examine the validity of these claims. Our concern here is to understand the Marxian methodology of History with the sole object of discovering a suitable method for the composition of Indian history with all the uniqueness and the generality it connotes and all the responsibility it throws on its renewal.

The number of experts who have thrown light on different aspects of Marxism is very large. While a library could be filled with volumes and essays on its economics, politics, Dialectics and Historical Materialism, very little, in English at least, is available on the operative part of the method actually followed by Karl Marx, Engels, Lenin and other Marxists in their historical writings. (The difficulty is enhanced in India by the Government ban.) That part has been put under the blanket-term of Dialectics. The manner in which the word 'Dialectics' is used by some Marxists has, however, put a heavy discount on its effectiveness for explanation. The 'laws of Dialectics' have been made to behave like the laws of Karma—pre-determining every fact, event and human behaviour in its course ; or else, they are held forth as a moral justification for what is commonly described as opportunism. A careless use of 'laws', even if they be of 'Dialectics', does not save them from the fallacy involved in the reversal of the time-process implicit in the course of an argument ; a generalization arising out of and/or after the observation of data can hardly be seized, and if suspected, can only be very cautiously exploited before or even on the eve of the observation, however noble the purpose may be. On the other hand, without Dialectics Marxism hangs in the air, as it does, for example, by the magic wand of Max Eastman. (*Marxism : Is it Science ?* Part IV, sec. 2, and Part V). But we are referring to the social effectiveness of an explanation where we are sure that a recourse to the 'laws of Dialectics' will be helpful to clear thinking on the issue. So the author of this essay prefers to quote from the Marxist classics without detriment to Dialectics. His conclusions, from the very nature of the subject, cannot but be tentative. History is a going concern—despite the efforts of historians to close it by summing it up in their age and their views—this we know ; Marxism too is not a closed system in theory and practice—this we should know. No careful student of Marxism has taken it thus ; no important leader of action along Marxist lines has looked upon it as a dogma sufficient unto all days, without jeopardizing the cause he held dear. The two main platforms of Marxism are a certain understanding of History, Science, and a logic of change or changing functions. Each posits reality as a social process. So, a dogmatic application of this doctrine or that of Marx, Engels, Lenin, or Stalin is repugnant to the very premiss and method of Marxism. It is a form of *mala prohibitia.* Lenin, for example, had the honesty and courage to develop the hints of Marx and Engels, e.g. in the matter of Imperialism, dictatorship of the proletariat, organization of the party and Soviets ; Stalin has forged ahead of Lenin in regard to planning, peasantry and nationalities ; Mao has struck a hitherto unidentified vein of Marxism in the organization of a country which is simultaneously at all levels of material development. In other words, the following account of Marxian methodology in History will defeat its purpose if Marxism be taken as a gospel. The authority of the

Word is great everywhere, and particularly so in India ; hence the need of a warning.

And yet, the essentials of Marxism fix as it were ‘ the standard deviation ’. They differentiate the openness of the Marxist method of History from the subjective historical relativism of men like Dilthey and Troeltsch and their closed system of ‘ individual wholes’ no less than from the perfectionist seekers of Unity like Freeman and H. G. Wells who would make their learning and imagination override the diversity of ages and peoples, or the apologetic ones like Buckle or Toynbee* who would ultimately yield to a factor or a formula in quest of the same Unity. This demarcation from the different types of historical method is logically achieved in the following manner. In Marxism, ‘ the limits of approximation of our knowledge to the objective, absolute truth are historically conditional, but the existence of such truth is unconditional, and the fact that we are approaching nearer to it is unconditional.’ In these words Lenin (*Materialism and Empirio-Criticism*) has summed up the Marxist differentiation which Engels had fully enunciated in Chapter X on Morality and Law : Eternal Truths, in his *Anti-Duhring*, (particularly pp. 99-105—Marxist-Leninist Library). The limits of historical knowledge, which is one aspect of the knowledge of objective truth, are set by the critical appreciation of forces behind the recorded and the noticeable facts, including theories of history, society, ideas, etc. For Marxism, records and chronicles are only the tail-ends of events ; forces posit human behaviour for ends, ideals, values and purposes ; know-

*Toynbee's method is treated in a subsequent chapter.

ledge involves activity and experiment to distinguish it from dogma ; history indicates direction by human ends, etc., the choice of which is mainly governed by the interests of the dominant economic group. The constellation of these forces forms the design of a historical situation, i.e. the history of a country at a given stage of material development in the *milieu* of its conditions and relations of production and the resulting disposition of classes. This necessarily means that the Marxist conception of History is not that of a Unity, say as that of Freeman, who in his famous Rede lecture propounded the thesis that 'As man is the same in all ages, the history of man is one in all ages.' At the same time, the 'unconditional' nature of approximating or 'approaching' supplies the dynamic element of unity in the Marxist method. The process of approximating is through the conflict of classes, which is the human counterpart of the conflict between new forces of production and the older vestiges of conditions and relations. Production, in its forces, conditions and relations,* therefore, touches the whole gamut of human living, with living on the material plane as the key-note, the standard *swara* or the *vadi*. In the natural sciences, for example, the approximation of knowledge is towards an unconditional, objectively existing model ; but in History no such model exists. Historically conscious men may be loosely said to be behaving *as if*

*Marx uses the term '*Productions-Verhältnisse*', i.e. relations of production to denote how '*Productive-Kräfte*', i.e. forces of production, and '*Productions-Bedingungen*', i.e. conditions of production, are socially organized by human activity. Culture etc. is conditioned by the 'relations', not by 'forces' and 'conditions' of production. See Engels' letter to Starkenburg, Jan. 25, 1894.

such a model existed. But that would not be methodologically Marxist, although it would be sanctioned by the logic of the anarchist notion of historical change or of Utopian Socialism.

Is then the Marxist view not objective because it can have no 'objectively existing model'? There is a distinction between the approaches of an objectivist historian and a Marxist historian. The Marxist, not being content with speaking of the necessity of a determined historical process made up of 'irrefragable historical tendencies', or of patterns of events held objectively by their own relevance and causation, investigates the given socio-economic complex and lays bare the content of the process, the interest-group dominating that complex and the forms of opposition to it by other groups, in short, the class-antagonism. The result is that while the objectivist historian can look at History as from the royal box in a theatre, the Marxist historian suggests that in the evaluation of events an 'objective' account is incomplete on the very ground of its neutrality, and complete by self-inclusion into the object of evaluation. This is the methodological significance of 'taking sides' which, Lenin said, was the clear duty of the materialist, i.e. the Marxist historian.

Still we are far away from Science. In fact, 'self-inclusion', 'taking sides'—such phrases seem to take us away from Science instead of bringing us nearer to it. Quite the contrary. We will see in the following argument that we thus come only closer to scientific method in regard to the meaning of History.

'Men make their own history, but not just as they please,' wrote Marx; and for Engels, History is 'the activity of man in pursuit of his ends'. As activity without ends or ideals is inconceivable, so also the ends when reached or the ideals when achieved, that is to say, historical effects, which alone are recorded or chronicled, are inexplicable solely in terms of ends or ideals. The reason is that the process involves the complicated interaction of individual wills, and of the physical and the human including the 'technic' environments. As Engels puts it: 'The history of social development is essentially different in one respect from that of nature. In nature—in so far as we disregard the reaction of man upon it—there exist only unconscious, blind agents which influence one another and through whose reciprocal interplay general laws assert themselves. Whatever occurs . . . does not occur as a consciously willed end. On the other hand, in social history the active agents are always endowed with consciousness, are always men working towards definite ends with thought and passion. Nothing occurs without conscious intent, without willed end. But this difference, important as it may be for historical investigation . . . does not alter the fact that the course of history obeys general laws. For here, too, on the surface, despite the consciously willed ends of individuals, chance seems to rule. Only seldom does that occur which is willed. In most cases the numerous ends which are willed conflict with or cut across one another, or they are doomed from the very outset to be unattainable, or the means to carry them out are insufficient. And so, out of the conflicts of innumerable individual wills and acts there arises in the social world a situation which is quite analogous to that in the unconscious, natural one. The ends of action are willed; but the results, which really flow from those actions, are not willed, or, in so far as the results seem to agree with the willed ends, ultimately they turn out to be quite other than the desired consequence.' (Engels' *Feurbach*)

The above quotation has to be studied carefully to appreciate how in spite of the difference between History and the Natural Sciences, the wide variety of results and their 'otherness' from the willed ends, the Marxist methodology of History is scientific. Engels speaks of 'one respect'; in other respects, e.g., observation and its accuracy, the use of hypotheses and formulae at a certain stage of enquiry, the elaboration and condensation of data, their description into manageable forms, the search for connexions, etc., (Langlois and Seignobos—*An Introduction to the Study of History*, p. 264), the study of History and the study of Nature may be said to be on all fours. And then Engels uses the word Science as Feurbach had used it, viz. in the sense of Physics and Chemistry. In other books, as in *Anti-Duhring* and *Dialectics of Nature*, Engels, who was deeply interested in scientific development in various fields, pointed out the difference between Physics, Chemistry, and Biology. Today, Science also includes Biology, particularly, in its aspects of Evolution. Unless we choose to dismiss Darwin, Mendel, Bateson from the rosters of Science, we will have to admit that History, as Marx and Engels understood it, belongs to that very respectable group of sciences, beginning with Astronomy and ending in Biology, which, in the language of Miss Stebbing (*A Modern Introduction to Logic*, p. 376) 'cannot omit the time-direction'. The 'otherness' of results from willed ends is also not to be taken as an argument against the treatment of History as a science. 'Otherness' only suggests, to quote Miss Stebbing again in criticism of Jevons' similar charge, that 'historical knowledge does not take the form of abstract generalizations about repeatable events'.

The 'numerous ends' and the 'innumerable individual wills', if left to themselves, would be certainly antagonistic to scientific treatment. But, usually, they are grouped into classes, according to the Marxist. They have also a direction, dictated by class-ends and interests. As such, they have a regularity (not recurrence). Being possessed of these qualities, they can be compared, correlated and contrasted, and their movement can be charted with a fair measure of accuracy. So the enormity of variation and number only indicates that the mathematical basis of that variety of Science to which History may be said to belong is not arithmetical, but statistical. Marxian method of History would not, however, advise the application of continuous curves. Their application often leads to ludicrous results, although the origin may be in aesthetic pleasure. (Morris Cohen—*Reason and Nature*, p. 353-4) But while we are more or less aware of the limited applicability of statistics in History we also know that this defectiveness really arises from the smallness of the number of instances taken. Engels speaks of very large numbers. So, logically, the largeness itself should correct the errors. (See the statistical analysis and charts in Pitrim Sorokin's *The Crisis of Our Age.* Sorokin is anti-Marxist.) The greater the number and the diversity, the greater is the statistical regularity and the more restricted is the play of chance. We know how many 'accurate' sciences (those which have omitted time-direction) are being re-based upon new theories and 'time-understanding', i.e. historical understanding as they all must be. Still we must not overdraw on Statistics. The logic of 'probability' must needs posit some 'determinate ratio to begin with'; and the logic of mathematical calculation, which subsumes statistics, enables us to 'pass from a small number of instances to an indefinitely large number by the process of summation or integration';—these assumptions, no History, however statistical its method may be, can provide, nor is expected to provide. We must not also forget that no rigorously statistical treatment of History can yield us a set of 'average motives' deduced from mass behaviour on the line of 'statistical constants'. Many historians, political thinkers, economists and sociologists, without the help of statistics, have no doubt discovered them. They have thereby reduced the historical process to the play of heroes or of the economic man, of Imitation, Conflict, Co-operation, and of similar abstractions of which Henry Wallace's Common Man, probably the issue of the Unknown Soldier of the last Great War, is the latest. Even Karl Liebknecht wanted to discover 'average material motives' in his attempt to make Marx more scientific. His 'average material motives' only made up the old economic man in 'red' guise. Marx's subject in History was the whole man, whose integrity was jeopardized by class-divisions and could be restored by their liquidation.

Another important point to note in Engels' paragraph is the qualification of the word 'chance'. On the 'surface' only chance 'seems' to rule. In reality, 'chance' does not *rule*. Chance, both in modern science and in Marxism, arises not because Nature and History are outside the pale of rationality or causality and belong to the realm of blind forces, but in the following circumstances: (a) When all the steps in the connexion are not known and fully measured, as we expect them to be in order that we may think that the final result is pre-determined ; (b) when the range of possible antecedents is unconsciously or consciously limited by the observer, and the conclusion is not borne out in one to one—or one to any whole number—relation to the preceding links in the selected field of causation ; and (c) when a particular group of antecedent phenomena which seem to have behaved autonomously for some considerable time begin to swim into the observer's ken like a new star or a constellation. Unless 'chance' is equivalent to irrelevance, it must be related to some aspect in causation or to some law. Again, it could not be all chance and no law, for that would be a denial of the logical process itself. Within this ambit, the so-called 'chance' operates. Chance cannot function independently of the whole set of antecedent factors. Lenin is not chance, nor is Gandhiji. In collaboration with the whole set, the influence of chance-elements functions 'within a narrow range of possibilities conditioned by an antecedent state of affairs'. So, the importance of 'chance', both for Marxian History and Science, consists in its being a corrective of crude determinism. Marx is very clear on this point. In his letter to Kugelmann (April 12, 1871), he writes.: 'Its (world history's) nature would have to be of a very mystical kind if "accidents" played no role. These accidents naturally fall within the general path of development and are compensated by other accidents. But the acceleration and retardation of events are very largely dependent upon such "accidents" among which must be reckoned the character of the people who stand at the head of the movement.' (For a fuller discussion of the relation between chance and necessity see Engels' *Dialectics of*

Nature—pp. 230-34 of the notes in the Marxist-Leninist Library translated and edited by Clemens Dutt; Engels' letter to Hans Starkenburg, Jan. 25, 1894, sec. 2(b); Marx's letter to Kugelmann April 12, 1871.) The usual conception of leadership is vitiated by a misunderstanding about the nature of chance caused by re-action against a naive faith in the mechanistic explanation of data, events and human activity. Without 'X' things would have been otherwise; with 'X' things are what they are. But 'X' himself can be 'X' i.e., he can function decisively only within a limited range of possibilities and in collaboration with them. 'X' is a manifestation of a tendency, and in his turn, affects the tendency in a limited way. Once this is understood, room for the worship of leaders becomes restricted.*

The cardinal point in the quotation from Engels is the clause 'in so far as we disregard the reaction of man on it (nature)'. It was necessary to rebut Feurbach's mechanistic materialism which allotted no place to individual acts, wills, ends, and ideals. (Feurbach ascribed the Irish subjection to England to potatoes and prescribed beans as a change.) Engels' and Marx's view of nature is that the reaction of man on nature cannot be disregarded. "Physical nature, indeed, exerts a direct effect upon world history"—wrote Hegel in his Philosophy of History. For Marx, its effect is indirect, i.e., only in so far as it enters into material production which is a double process, viz., (a) between man and nature, and (b) between men and men (Holy Family). In Marxist thought nature is never the pure nature of Physical Geography. It is closer to the nature of Human

*The question of personality is treated in a subsequent chapter.

Geography. In reality, nature may be said to belong to 'material' production, because that is how Marx understands nature. Even the "laws of nature" are for Marx "social laws of nature", and society is a pattern of material forces, conditions and relations.

III

The conclusion that emerges from the above is that in spite of the one essential difference between the history of social development and of nature, the Marxist historian considers it legitimate to include History within Science, i.e., one type of sciences. Since the days of Marx and Engels, the logic of scientific experiment has gone ahead ; and it supports the above conclusion in so far as the mechanistic view of nature against which it was historically necessary for Dilthey to posit *Geisteswissenschaft* has been abandoned by the scientists themselves. This changed position of Science has brought History and Science closer than before. Edgar Wind, for example, has lodged his objection against Dilthey's claim for the autonomy of History on the ground of the intrusion of the observer. In an able contribution to the Essays presented to Ernst Cassirer (*Philosophy and History*—Edited by Klibansky, pp. 255-264) he shows how the scientist and the historian work on the same line. 'Generally speaking this might be termed the dialectic of the historical document—that the information which one tries to gain with the help of the document ought to be presupposed for its adequate understanding. The scientist is subject to the same paradox. The physicist seeks to infer general laws of nature by instruments themselves subject to these laws.' The presupposition in either case looks like reasoning in a circle.

Actually, it is not circular, but dialectical. An absence of pre-supposition throws both the scientist and the historian into the mercy of chaos. There are also cases of slides tucked away in the cupboard by a laboratory assistant and of manuscripts in a tin-box until they are discovered with ecstasy by men with pre-suppositions. Again, any future historian of India in the twentieth century will surely go to the files of *Young India* and the *Harijan* as documents for India's history, and equally surely find there, at the same time, the part played by Gandhiji in that period. But why should these two papers be selected in preference to others unless there be some pre-supposition ? Here the document will have been used no longer as means but as the object of inquiry. Such a dialectical shift of focus from means to ends is apt to be missed by the experimenter, but it is happening always in the laboratory. Previously, we have used the word 'self-inclusion' as the significance of 'taking sides' by which Lenin distinguished the objectivist from the materialist, i.e., the Marxist historian. Here, at last, we see that the process is implicit in the scientific method itself. In criticizing Dilthey's 'inward', 'immediate', 'intuitive' apprehension of the socio-historical reality by the agents themselves, (through their being themselves, as individuals, elements in the interactions of that socio-historical reality which is to be studied), Edgar Wind also points out that apart from being a bold assertion such inwardness reduces the Kantian moral precept into the status of a fact or a process which is not borne out either by experience or by the psychology of the Unconscious. For example, the future historian of the India of 1942 will certainly find it difficult to grasp the connexion between the text of the August resolution of the Congress and Gandhiji's statement in 1944 thereupon, on the one hand, and the disturbances as 'open rebellion', on the other. It is a different matter if the historian discards his scientific attitude, which must needs proceed by documents, in favour of a moral precept to be interpreted by intuition, which is not so dependent on documents and science. On another level, viz., that of the *status quo* or of make-believe, unfortunately, not also scientific, and yet equally human, the historian may put the two together as cause and effect. The point is that the historian often works on two levels of consciousness, the scientific and the intuitive-moral, because to produce a total picture he finds it awkward to ignore either. Dilthey's claim for the autonomy of the historical method does not yield the secret of the combination of the two, but only segregates them without guarding against the dangers of dichotomisation, like that of letter and spirit, which as we know covers a moral judgement instead of stating a conclusion. On the other hand, a little analysis shows that Dilthey's plea, stripped of its profundity, means, in the language of E. Wind, '*The investigator intrudes into the process that he is investigating*' (Italics Wind's), a fact which is just as much true of the historian as it is of the physicist, because it is demanded by the rules of the game itself. An investigator, be he in the laboratory or in the archive, must be historically conditioned towards the instruments and the records to be able to register signs, signals, significance ; he must co-ordinate them, select them round about a hypothesis. In the study of history, the data being comparatively smaller in quantity in the relatively unknown periods, and also being unrepeatable by nature, hypotheses tend to get mixed up with motives. But this only calls for greater caution which, as we know, is provided by grammatical and critical axioms of hermeneutics. So the separation is not of the order of body and soul in medieval theology, Government and the people in British India, or say, the Communist and the nationalist in today's frustrated India, but of the order of part and whole by the common fact of intrusion. 'By this intrusion into the process that is to be studied, the student himself, like every one of his tools, becomes part-object of investigation ; "part-object" to be taken in a two-fold sense ; he is, like any other organ of investigation, but a part of the whole object that is being investigated. But equally it is only a part of himself that, thus externalized into an instrument, enters into the object-world of his studies.' (Wind) Of course, there may be extreme cases of identification, such as a zoologist's behaving like a worm, a slide, or a microscope, and a historian's like Lorenzo de Medici, a copper-plate, or a palm-leaf manuscript ; but the progress of Science and History does not lean heavily on the sincerity of such scholars. (An actor who is so completely objective as to be at one with his part is laughed at. At least, that is the author's experience as one of the audience. Art too, it seems, cannot admit Dilthey's claim.)

It is obvious that the intrusion is of one who knows the rules of the game. The critical axioms are a 'part of the experimental hypothesis', otherwise the intruder is like the villager come to town. The trained intruder must avoid collisions with errors, reject the hypothesis he has been working upon in order to make himself ready to accept a new one more suitable for the new occasion. Intrusion brings in errors, but rejection of errors is also not feasible except by trained intrusion. Both the historian and the scientist intrude in this way into investigation. After all, Science and History proceed not from truth to truth, but in tortuous ways wading through errors as well. For which, their methodology will have to have a theory which is not just good enough for truth and/or for any one cross-section of investigation ; it will have to provide for a theory of errors implicit in the process of investigation.

The result of trained intrusion is transformation, because 'this intrusion . . . is a thoroughly real event'. A Raman disturbs atoms when he sets up an instrument, a Shah does likewise to the nexus of nature when he studies the Sun or a Bhaba the cosmic rays. Similarly, a Shyam Sastri reconstructs modern India when he discovers the Arthasastra and proclaims its importance for ancient India. An investigator disturbs the dust of centuries and the silence of nature, and his investigation changes the tools and implements, just as changes in the latter help the investigator. Investigation as such is an exchange from which the intruder cannot be excluded without peril to its progress. It means transformation of facts into events, and of a Grandgrind into a historian. 'History can be events' as M. Berr said, but only in this sense. The scientist and the historian have always 'taken sides' ; they will, in days to come ; because the process of exchange, transformation, 'making' is never-ending. It is high time that the dialectics of investigation were better known than what they are today. The idea of 'making history' will not appear so irrelevant as it is to the 'scientific' historian.

IV

An important corollary to the Marxian methodology, as the author has understood it, is the recognition of the fact of crisis which marks the beginning no less than the end of an epoch. The epochal character of History operates within the limits of at least these two major facets of each crisis. The actual operation of the historical process is in terms of conflict and maturity. The conflict is between the material forces of production at a certain stage of development and the existing conditions of production or, juristically, with the system of property under which they have been functioning so long. Marx's conception of maturity is governed by a few major considerations : (a) It is not to be evaluated in terms of consciousness ; but, at least, in one aspect, viz., the changes in the conditions of production, it can be gauged scientifically. Marx writes in the Introduction to the *Critique of Political Economy* : 'As little as an individual can be judged from the opinion he has of himself, just as little can a revolution be judged from men's consciousness of it. On the contrary, this consciousness is to be explained between the social forces of production and the conditions of production.' Marx writes further : 'In order to understand such a revolution it is necessary to distinguish between the changes in the conditions of economic (Marx does not use the word 'material' here) production which are a material fact and can be observed and determined with the precision of natural science, on one hand, and on the other, the legal, political, religious, artistic and philosophic—in short, ideological forms in which men become conscious of this conflict and fight it out.' This latter side of the conflict was not logically or historically treated by Marx, as he had not the time to do it ; it was practised in his various historical writings, e.g. *the Eighteenth Brumaire, Civil War in France, Class Struggle in France*, where the influence of political forms is brilliantly brought out. Two letters of Engels, one to J. Bloch, September 21, 1890 and the other to F. Mehring, July 14, 1893, refer to the reasons for this lapse. Above all, there is the whole life of Marx to show conclusively the importance of the ideological forms of conflict in the Marxist method. Every Marxist must needs wage these conflicts in his active life. (b) Marx puts the case for maturity (Lenin's 'revolutionary situation') in the context of the forces of production and material necessity. Says he : 'No form of society can perish before all the forces of production which it is large enough to contain are developed, and at no time will outworn conditions be replaced by new higher conditions as long as the material necessities for their existence have not been hatched in the womb of the society itself.' It is well known how Lenin always emphasized this dialectical play of two forces setting the limits of a revolutionary situation, its start and its potentiality, on the one hand, and the existing order's strength and weakness, on the other. (c) Lest the above may appear too abstract and transcendental, Marx hastened to add that 'mankind never sets itself a problem that it cannot solve', the possibility of the solution, however, depending upon either existing or developing 'material' (not economic) 'conditions' (not forces). (d) Conflict (leading to crisis) is not, therefore, a philosopher's concept. Its limits, its aspects, its two-fold functions are human and material, i.e., social and historical. If we use the word loosely, these two 'forces' are represented in two social classes in opposition. Such an opposition is the chief motive power of any considerable historical movement. Here maturity is left by Karl Marx in the hand of the class-conscious proletariat. There are few details, however, in Marx's own writings about the theoretical side of this process of maturing. The practical aspect, however, does not concern us here, although we must point out that it is the more important of the two. (e) There is another opposition mentioned by Karl Marx, but which has been unfortunately neglected by the general run of the Marxist theoretician, viz., that between the town and the country. Says Karl Marx in Vol. I of *Capital*: 'The whole economic history of society is summed up in the movement of this antagonism.' Like the first, this antagonism too needs maturing. Here also the matter was not pushed to its theoretical limits.

Therefore, Marx's historical methodology is scientific primarily in its avoidance of (a) conceptual abstractions—the defect of the Idealist Schools of Historians, and (b) mechanical causation—the bane of the purely materialist school and its progeny, viz., the 'scientific historians' who would deal with 'facts and nothing but facts'. It is essentially scientific (a) in its understanding of the subject-matter of history, viz., social process and movement, (b) in its attempt at the discovery of specific tendencies by means of which the direction of the process may be indicated, its intensity appraised, and quality formulated, and (c) in its emphasis upon the practical, the empirical and the instrumental, which has always been the initial and the ultimate drive of all sciences. To establish this scientific method in history, Marx recognizes the convenience of fixing at a time upon one social force, one category and of relating it to its specific, historical epoch, and subsequently, by the urgency of the subject and the deed, of pushing backward and forward to suggest a Unity of History made of unities or specificities of histories. This specificity in the case of Marx was Capitalism, the dominant institution of the contemporary epoch, the contradictions of which Ricardo had noticed, but which Marx noticed and utilized by means of his theoretical analysis as the agency for precipitating the crisis.

Nobody need or can identify this approach with that involved in the theory of Kultur-Kreise with its concrete. individual whole, its ramifications in the learned doctrines of Culture as a 'unity of teleological tendencies' or of History as the 'story of living experience' or of History to be 'intuitively divined in a flash'. Benedetto Croce (*Historical Materialism and the Economics of Karl Marx*), Max Eastman, (*Marxism : Is It Science ?*) and a lesser known writer but a learned one, Karl Federn (*The Materialist Conception of History*), therefore, are wrong in their interpretations of the historical methodology of Karl Marx. Trotsky's view of History as Unity, as in his Theory of World Revolution, is essentially non-Marxist in its haughty neglect of the specificities of epochs, cultural traits and material progress. Lenin's interpretation is the same as that of his master except in his refinement of the method of bringing about the crisis. He too discusses Russian Capitalism and relates Imperialism to a specific historical epoch, contemporary again, whose main feature he described as monopoly, finance-capital.

V

We have used the word, 'specificities' above. Prof. Karl Korsch in his study of Marx in the series on Modern Sociologists (Chapts. II & III) considers 'the principle of historical specification' to be the essence of the Marxian method. In the following paragraphs we have followed, and developed his analysis.

(1) Marx spent a great deal of his intellectual energy in discussing 'value' because his predecessors had taken 'value' as a category true for all time. For Marx, this concept, 'although an abstraction, is an *historical* abstraction which, therefore, could only be made on the basis of a *determinate* economic development of society.' (Marx's letter to Engels, April 2, 1858)

(2) The various forms of Rent and Capital in Marx's writings are still more intimately (positively) connected with historical stages and epochs of social development. The wealth of historical learning displayed in unravelling the threads of their intricate connexion remains unsurpassed. The cue is given in *The Poverty of Philosophy* (p. 135) where Marx writes: 'Ricardo, after postulating bourgeois production as necessary for determining rent, applies the conception of rent, nevertheless, to the landed property of all ages and all countries. This is an error common to all the economists, who represent the bourgeois relations of production as eternal categories.' Elsewhere in the same book (p. 88) Marx quotes Proudhon as writing 'We are not giving a history according to the order in time, but according to the sequence of ideas,' and comments: 'Economists explain how production takes place in the above-mentioned relations, but what they do not explain is how these relations themselves are produced,

that is, the *historical movement* which gave them birth.' In *Capital* (Vol. III), written later, Rent is '*a specific historical* form into which feudal landownership and small peasant's agriculture have been transformed through the influence of capital and of the capitalistic mode of production.'

(3) Similarly, it is only the appearance of '*definite historical conditions*' which can make things, objects, products into commodities, govern the form and content of exchange, and account for the different types of money and their social functions. (*Capital*, Vol. I, Chs. 1, 2, 3.)

(4) Nowhere is historical specificity more implicit than in Marx's treatment of Capital, e.g., Capital for trading in goods, capital for trading in money, capital for lending money. Each is the dominant trait of capital in an historical epoch, and one is transformed into the other as the socio-economic evolution proceeds. But the transformation is historical ; i.e., no historical form disappears ; the vestiges remain. Lenin brilliantly followed Marxian methodology in his history of Capitalism in Russia and in his study of Imperialism as the latest, contemporary stage of Capitalism.

(5) Nowhere also does Marx take himself as an economic historian, like Cunningham, Lipson or Clapham of England. We look in vain for a descriptive account of the economic history of a country from the earliest time to the day when Marx wrote. (Engels' *Peasant's War* like his *Origin of the Family* etc. is a dip into the past, but for a highly contemporary purpose.) Edmund Wilson has called Marx 'the poet of commodities'. It is a brilliant statement worthy of one who can interpret Marxian economics and politics

through the symbols in Marx's youthful adventures in poetry. But apart from *Capital,* to which the above *bon mot* is applied, Edmund Wilson's estimate of Marx's historical writings comes very near the heart of the Marxian method. In contrast to the French historians, and Michelet is one of them, who were 'perplexed by the confused and complex series of changes' happening in France, Marx 'provides a chart of the currents' ....which completely overthrows 'the traditional revolutionary language made up of general slogans and abstract concepts........' 'Nowhere perhaps in the history of thought is the reader so made to feel excitement of a new intellectual discovery.' (E. Wilson—*To the Finland Station*, p. 201) We no doubt get the most penetrating account of money, commodities, division of labour, and of numerous other concepts; but the occasion is always to show their epochal nature, i.e., the qualities of each in its social, economic and historical setting; and the purpose is to bring out their significance in the present contemporary context in order that action may be taken with full understanding and responsibility, if such action were desirable, as Karl Marx along with many others before and after his time thought that it was. (Thus far Prof. Korsch.)

(6) Marx's close interest in contemporary affairs is well-known. To him, as to few historians, Croce's remark that all history is contemporary history is applicable. He would read reports, meet agents, attend secret and open conferences to judge and direct revolutionary movements in the various countries of Europe. After his death Engels found two whole cubic metres of Russian statistical materials alone in Marx's none too spacious rooms. His highly developed sense of

'living time' is itself an instance of his approach by 'specification'. At the same time, his feeling for the contemporariness of History made ample allowance for the diversities in historical situations. It is not submitted, however, that his reading of them was always infallible; nor can one dogmatically maintain that in view of his primary interest in removing the evils of autocracy then typified by Russia, or of the evils of Capitalism in Germany and England, he was never led to behave or to advise in a manner which could be construed to rest upon the pre-supposition of an overriding, homogeneous, i.e., non-specific, and eternal law of social development and History. His stirring call to the workmen of all nations to unite and his interest in the First International are two cases which easily jump into one's mind. And yet, a scrutiny of Karl Marx's writings, speeches and his guidance of the movements in different countries of Europe would reveal where his emphasis lay. Thus England's case was essentially different from that of Russia. As it is probably not permissible to quote the full text of Karl Marx's speech at Amsterdam after the Hague Congress, Engels' Foreword to the English translation of Karl Marx's *Capital* may be quoted instead: 'Surely, at such a moment the voice ought to be heard of a man whose theory is the result of a life-long study of the economic conditions of England, and whom that study led to the conclusion that at least in Europe, England is the only country where the inevitable social revolution might be effected entirely by peaceful and legal means. He certainly never forgot to add that he hardly expected the English ruling classes to submit, without a "pro-slavery rebellion," to this peaceful and legal revolution.'

But about Russia Karl Marx's views were otherwise. Recent researches have demolished the dishonest conclusion that according to Marx Russia should have been the last country to achieve a revolution and that it was all Lenin's doing without reference to the Marxian methodology. During the last ten years of Karl Marx's life great things were happening in Russia. His Russian studies, which would form the material of his theoretical discussion on ground rent in the Vol. II of *Capital* just as his English studies had formed the basis of his theoretical argument on capitalism in Vol. I, forced him to conclude that Russia was a colossus with feet of clay. In 1877, Russia declared war on Turkey, and Marx was sure of the collapse of Czardom to be followed by a revolution. In Sept. 1877, he wrote to Sorge : 'All classes of Russian society are economically, morally, intellectually in complete decay.... This time the revolution will begin in the East.' Next year, on Feb. 4, Marx wrote to Liebknecht of the reasons for his sympathy for the Turks against Russians : '(i) because we have studied the Turkish peasant, i.e. the Turkish masses, and we have learnt that the Turkish peasant is without doubt one of the most capable and moral representatives of European peasantry ; (ii) because the defeat of the Russians will considerably hasten the social revolution in Russia, the elements of which already to great extent exist, and thereby also hasten the revolutions in all Europe.' In 1879-1880 several abortive attempts were made on the life of the Czar, and Marx seemed to feel that the Terror was a historically inevitable means of action for Russia. After Karl Marx, Engels continued to believe that the revolutionists in Russia were on the 'eve of victory'. Lenin's attitude towards Czarist Russia as the bulwark of all reactionary forces and his weakness for the Old Guard of revolutionaries are too well known to need elaboration here.

(7) Probably the best example of the Marxist method in history is to be found in the approach towards the problem of nationalities in the U.S.S.R. It is well known how the different nationalities were first classified into three categories in accordance with their levels of material development, which, in the Marxian sense, also signifies territory, culture, psychological make-up, etc. The world also knows how in the midst of the war, but not solely by the war, these nationalities have forged a unity which can easily admit of the nearly complete specification of each constituent nationality even to the extent of keeping its own political and military distinctness. Be it noted that the political, military and cultural forms making up the specification are in their structural pattern only the conditions and relations of material production ; if they vary, they do so as the forces and the conditions of material production in these units differ between themselves ; and so, if they tend to unite, it is at the instance of the same material agencies working for a design of approximating unity, probably, now on the level of 'relations' rather than under any bureaucratic impulse. Methodologically, therefore, the solution of the practical problem of nationality-cultures is dependent upon a view of History different from that of the idealist or the mechanical-materialist historians. One wonders what Trotsky who combined the vices of both schools of History would have done with the problem of nationalities. Probably not better than what is being done in this land of preaching idealists and practising materialists.

Lest there be any misunderstanding about the word 'specification', it is to be pointed out that it is not the 'specification' of engineers for contractors to satisfy. Nor is it identical with the 'type' of typologists like Max Weber. It is poles asunder from the ethos of the school of historians at the initial flush of the romantic-nationalist movement (Fichte) or at its period of frustration (Spengler). We know too well the defects of these schools; their undefined types, the neglect of cross-types, the arbitrary assumptions in regard to the constituent elements of types and the 'intuitive' understanding of their genius, spirit, etc., their susceptibility to interpretation in the light of the motive for perpetuating vested interests by the powers themselves who alone can interpret the 'soul' of the type and do so to curb opposition and change, their inability to frame a world-picture in any sense other than the cyclical and the repetitive, etc., etc. Marxian method steers clear of these defects. At the same time, there is the unmistakable emphasis on the dominant, therefore, the distinguishing trait of an epoch. Material trait it undoubtedly is; but material in the socio-historical sense, including the 'relations': But dominant it must also be by virtue of the combination of the following features of the trait: It has a structural unity, a *gestalt*, which is always tending to give a form to the subordinate parts; (as such it may be called primary and others secondary, the relation being similar to, but not identical with, an object and its reflection or image, in the older language of psychology;) it has the quality of emergence which from the earlier premiss involves discontinuity but may appear as an analogue to the earlier form (Marx's 'calling up of the dead', 'masquerading', 'parody', 'walking of the ghost of the old revolution'—*The Eighteenth Brumaire*); it is an instrument for criticism and change, thus possessing an element of activism (B. Russel would call it 'instrumentalism'—*Freedom and Organization*); and above all, it registers an advance not in the linear way which demands the prediction of the future dominant trait from the present one. (N. B. Neither for Marx nor for Engels is Communism, future or primitive, used as a positive historical statement but as means for historical change or investigation, i.e., in a dialectical manner making allowance for unequal tempo, other conditions, and regression.) Certain anthropologists, e.g. Ruth Benedict in her *Patterns of Culture*, speak about the stubbornness of the core of culture in the midst of pressure. The Marxist 'specification' may also be compared to the relative permanence, the comparative obduracy of a culture-pattern. For Marx, Capitalism is that contemporary pattern; its technology, its class-relations, its concepts of value, profit, its ideologies—are the traits and their features. Again, we must not push the comparison too far--only note the fruitfulness of the method and its scientific *bona fide* in the study of human affairs. The author, therefore, strongly feels that with the help of Marxist methodology the specificity of Indian History will be fully respected, its development and its contribution to the evolving World-History fairly indicated. And these are the ends which every Indian wills and to which every Indian Historian may easily subscribe without loss of intellectual honesty and dignity.

VI

Now the whole point of this essay will be missed if we forget that our main interest as Indians of this century and at this crisis of the world is not to write new volumes on Indian History for the sake of writing, or for the sake of flattering our national. communal, or sectarian prejudices. *Our sole interest is to write and to act Indian History.* Action means making ; it has a starting point—this specificity called India ; or if that be too vague, this specificity of the contact between India and England or the West. Making involves changing, which in its turn requires (a) a scientific study of the tendencies which make up this specificity, and (b) a deep understanding of the Crisis. In all these matters, the Marxian method, as the author of this essay has understood it, is likely to be more useful than other methods. If it is not, it can be discarded. After all, the object survives.

The author is not oblivious of the difficulties implicit in his suggestion. He is aware of the theoretical ones which philosophers, historians, logicians, economists, sociologists, and publicists have pointed out. (If a personal remark were permitted, the author has been trained and saturated in non-Marxist, anti-Marxist methodology in History, Economics and Sociology.) But he feels that the need of the contemporary situation calls for the trial of an approach to Indian History different from what has been made so far. If the need for a new India, i.e., for a free and genuinely democratic India, made up of nationalities, peoples and personalities, all unfettered by economic, social, political and historical shackles, be great ; if historians, being Indians and human beings, have a part to play in the shaping of their country and contributing to the welfare of the world ; if Indian Culture can be called 'specific' ; and lastly, if this crisis be a golden opportunity and not an occasion for despair, then the Marxist approach may be given a trial by our historians. For aught one knows, the theoretical difficulties are not insuperable, because they seldom arise from any well-grounded and firmly grasped principles either of the Idealist school or of the mechanistic-scientific approach. Our usual historical competence is characterized by pains-taking thoroughness, and great regard for rules of evidence, but it is singularly free from any philosophy, logic and understanding of the social motives. So the theoretical difficulties in shedding a method and accepting another seem to be over-rated. They may appear after some acquaintance. In the meantime, they are mainly psychological. Indians are a spiritual people, Indian History is a story of spiritual struggle, and Marxism is materialism, so, how can they meet ? But historians, who are very rational creatures, may as well know that Indian spirituality is the thing to be proven, and not to be assumed. Once such question-begging is done away with, the meaning of Marxist, i.e. historical 'materialism' may be inquired into. If it is not sensualism or mechanism. but a name for the socio-historical process, the opposition to it may be reduced. Personal opposition may still persist. For example, the historian may be a religious person. In which case, the difficulty may be solved by not trying to think at all about India's future and writing her history.

The practical difficulties, however, should never be minimized. Facts and data are incomplete. No historian can do without facts, and neither an economic history of India nor a social history of the Indian people has been properly written. And here the danger of imposing Marxian method is great. Marxism, because of the popularity of its political programme and of the unscholarly impatience of its protagonists, has often been reduced into a closed system. And History is anything but closed. The question of 'Dialectics' is also crucial. One cannot open the pages of Engels' *Anti-Duhring* or of any classic, and apply the 'laws of Dialectics' to the composition of a volume on Indian History. At the same time, one can notice, if one cares, that in the evaluation of a document and its interpretation, the dialectical procedure is being actually adopted by the historian himself. So the practical difficulties in the adoption of Marxian methodology demand a very scrupulous attitude, in fact, a more scrupulous one than what the historians who believe in soul, spirit, *zeitgeist*, race, etc. have betrayed so far. A 'Critique' of Indian History is the supreme need of the day.

2. A HISTORIAN WITH SCIENTIFIC APPROACH

If I were to choose my favourite among the living historians writing in English today I would unhesitatingly mention Arnold Toynbee, the man who presides over the Royal Institute of International Affairs, who brings out the masterly annual surveys of the world's events with almost unfailing regularity and still finds time and energy to be the author of the monumental work called *A Study of History*. England has been singularly fortunate in her historians. Gibbon, Hume, Macaulay, what a sweep they had ! Stubbs, Hallam, Maitland, Acton, Lecky, Green, what stupendous learning they possessed ! Modern research may have corrected a detail or two in their accounts, but they remain very true in their essentials. I still go back to Carlyle to understand the significance of the fall of the Bastille, to Gibbon for the reasons of an empire's decline, to Stubbs for the patient, coral-like growth of Constitutions, and to Lecky for the unfolding of man's reason and the meaning and limitations of political democracy. In England, their giant-race is not yet dead. Trevelyan, Gooch, Fisher, Thompson and Toynbee among the seniors, Namiar, Young, and Brogan among the juniors are still there to carry on that great tradition. Probably, one misses a thing or two now, but the compensation is ample. History, so long as Toynbee is there, retains its encyclopædic character. Frankly speaking, I do not want to confuse History with Archaeology. For me, pardon my old-fashioned taste, History should move with the simplicity and dignity, the sweep and majesty of

Dhrupad. It should rise superior to details by making them yield their inner purpose to the general direction of events. Incidents and accidents are gossip ; they are frightfully interesting ; who but the prig does not like to know the love-affairs of Cæsar or Napoleon ? But I would like to go to Shakespeare instead of Plutarch for the first, and to an air-conditioned cinema-hall for the second. For the broad march of France's history, I would prefer to sit on the balcony and read Michelet, and for Rome, my moth-eaten, dog-eared volumes of Mommsen and Gibbon. In short, I believe in the orderly patterns that emerge out of the panorama of human activities, the conflict and the co-operation of wills of human beings, their hard knocks with nature and the consequences of their deeds and misdeeds, their hopes and aspirations—some frustrated and some others twisted beyond the recognition of dreamers—the rise and fall of their destiny, and above all, their types of behaviour so diverse in their specificity and yet so unifying in the grandeur of their contrapuntal harmony. My faith in History is fortified by Arnold Toynbee. He uncovers variety, but discovers the unity of living, the secret of which is Challenge and Response.

A few preliminary remarks on modern historical methods are necessary to bring out the specialty of Toynbee's approach. There are two schools of opinion in regard to the suitability of the scientific method for purposes of history. The main arguments of the first school which include a wide variety of historians are two : (i) Human beings, unlike natural phenomena, have wills of their own. These wills can change the course of events. Their multiplicity and the unpredictableness of their behaviour do not create the recurrence which is the first requisite for scientific calculation. (ii) In actual experience we notice that a particular country with a definite culture-pattern has a way of life, an outlook towards life's aims, a philosophy of its own. This *weltanschauung* is an imponderable quality, and it refuses to be analysed into component parts, as scientific proof must demand. And yet, the general outlook of a people is very much of a reality. So there is a tension between scientific explanation and an important historical reality. It cannot be resolved by the so-called scientific method. It can be done only by positing a new type of approach, viz. the intuitive, which alone can grasp the wholeness and the spirit of History, leaving the parts to the more pedestrian approach of scientific observation and the rest of it. This latter school is very popular in Germany.

On the other hand, the opposing school of thought, viz. that of orthodox scientific History, argues that although human wills are various, less tractable than matter and unpredictable and incomputable in their consequences, yet such facts do not wring the withers of the scientific method in History. After all, one can always draw a sort of statistical mean from the welter of human behaviour and conclude therefrom the general tendency of events, much in the way as the actuary does for the insurance tables. Men, no doubt, will not behave according to a simple graph of conduct, still they are a part and parcel of Nature which subsumes their special human nature, and as such, they are statistically tractable. In regard to the part played by the imponderable and the accidental elements in the evolution of social groups, it is held that closer scrutiny can and will unfold their amenability to laws. The scientific historian emphasizes the similarity of historical treatment with the physical inasmuch as both proceed with the patient collection of data, their shifting by rigorous analysis, the building up of tentative hypotheses and their final rejection or adoption in the light of new data. An extension of the above position means that the historian and the scientist, both, are ethically neutral and should remain contented with a bare indication of the general tendency.

Between these two schools. lies the modern scientific historian. He will not take History as a variant of novel-writing, nor will he put it in the category of the natural sciences, like Physics and Chemistry, as certain orthodox scientific historians have tried to do. Much rather would he apply the method of the biological sciences, like Botany and Zoology, in which the structure of a species is fixed by types and its function studied by the comparative and other inductive methods. It is in this wider sense of the science of living matter that Toynbee is a typically modern scientific historian. I notice the freshness of Biology in Toynbee's approach.

Let us follow him as best as we can through the six volumes of his monumental study of history, remembering of course, that the work is not yet complete. Toynbee begins his survey with what he calls the 'shimmer of relativity' in the foreground of historical thought. The discovery of this fact he expects to lead him to ascertaining 'the presence of some constant and absolute object of historical thought in the background'. The words 'constant' and 'absolute' may not appear quite scientific, but they merely convey what every scientist presumes in his search and strikes upon during its course. Toynbee's next step is to search for an 'intelligible field of historical study' that would avoid the local or the contemporary standpoint of the historian, i.e. the subject himself. This attitude of caution towards subjectivity and this selection of a field are the two primary postulates of science. Toynbee is very particular in pointing out the effect of the age upon the historian's outlook. I am not sure how far his advice on this point can be carried into practice. The liberalism of Fisher, for example, reacts well upon his treatment of the history of Europe in the seventeenth, eighteenth, and the first half of the nineteenth century, but makes its incidence unequal in regard to the later phases when liberalism, tied up in its own contradictions, appeared to be a doctrine of bygone days. Still, Toynbee's warning is very welcome. He then takes up the test-case of Great Britain, maps the larger field of which Great Britain is a part, and extends it further into space and time. His conclusion is that British history is narrower than world-history and shorter than that of the species of which it is a part. But the immediate background of the field of British history becomes the Western Society. That society, in its turn, is shown to belong to an older, but similar, society. Obviously, this is the method of Biology by which an individual is placed in the sub-species, the sub-species in the species and the species in the genus, in an ever-widening circle.

History, however, should go beyond morphology and also be a study of evolution. So Toynbee analyses continuity. That term, according to him, cannot imply that 'the mass, momentum, volume, velocity, and direction of the social stream of human life are constant', or nearly so. Some discernible continuity there is always to be found in all living, but more helpful to our knowledge of living than this truism is the discovery of the 'points of relative discontinuity in the ever-rolling system' which includes 'the rapids'. 'In other words,' Toynbee says, 'the concept of continuity is only significant as a symbolic mental background on which we can plot out our perceptions of discontinuity in all their actual variety and complexity. . . .' 'Let us apply,' Toynbee continues, 'this general observation concerning the study of life to the Study of History.' Anybody who has heard of the way in which the conflict between the wave and the quanta in modern Physics is sought to be synthesized will not consider the above general consideration to be at all unscientific.

The key-sentence just quoted fixes the structure of Toynbee's method. Its cardinal importance, to my mind, consists in his acute perception of the relative and the discontinuous, that is to say, of types of societies. Toynbee discusses the features of these types in great detail. Five of them are living, two are fossilized relics to which a few of the former can be affiliated, a few are analogues, and others remain unidentified. These social types are the 'social atoms', i.e. 'independent entities in the sense that each of them constitutes by itself an "intelligible field of historical study", but which at the same time are all representatives of a single species.' Toynbee does not stop here; he goes on to compare, contrast, and interpret the interaction of the types. Here also, Toynbee remains as scientific as say the zoologist is. In his opinion, 'such a rhythmic alternation between two activities—the collection of materials and their arrangement, the finding of facts and their interpretation is native to life.' Science and Thought are, therefore, native to History. Toynbee thus reaches the formula of

Challenge and Response, a formula which shares with such other interpretative generalizations in the natural sciences the qualities of comprehension, directness and simplicity. To sum up: Toynbee's contribution to historiography consists in (i) the selection of the intelligible field of observation, (ii) the fixation of types of 'social atoms', (iii) the extension of the field into the larger background, and (iv) interpretation by comparison and contrast to reach a more comprehensive unity.

I have already submitted that this method is as 'scientific' as that of Biology. Toynbee, be it noted however, is somewhat arbitrary in his typology. For him, historical movement does not go much beyond alternation of rhythm. So long as this series of volumes is not complete we are apt to consider that Toynbee's idea of movement is an over-simplification of History, Knowledge and Life, and that his formula of Challenge and Response is only a consequence of it. In spite of Toynbee's concern with the physical and the geographical environment in the shaping of history, the formula remains a psychological one. All that stupendous learning does not yield anything very material beyond a description of the processes of give and take, their continuities and discontinuities. Like the Unity or the Continuity of History, this formula too is 'an unimpeachable but not very illuminating truism'. Above all, does it help anybody in the business of making History? Formulas, no doubt, are generally useless in such matters. At first they focus, soon they impede. But surely there is a difference between (a) a conscious directing of the movement of a people by the people themselves in full or partial possession of the drives, impulses and forces behind the historical movement—a possession admitting of the use of phrases which now partake of the nature of symbols, and (b) a contemplation of the pageantry of the rise and fall of types of civilization from an academic balcony by a master-mind who marvellously interprets it as rhythm, as the play of Challenge and Response, for the benefit of his guests removed like him from the blood, sweat and tears involved in that procession. These six volumes are retrospective, and not prospective, because they are written by one for whom History has been already made ; they are meant for the contemplative, the 'philosophic' temper ; they are epical, not dramatic ; they are the spectacle envisioned by a Ulysses in the arms of Penelope, or by a Prospero who has come home from the enchanted isle; they are not instinct with the tragedy of Prometheus Bound to unbind himself or of the wounded Philoctetes heaving the bow ; they are *not* even informed by the tragic sense of Christian History's redemption of Man, or in contrast, by Marxian History's redemption of the masses. One cannot think of Lenin or Jawaharlal turning over the pages of Toynbee's Scientific History in their years of exile or prison-life.

3. MYTHOLOGY AND THE BEGINNINGS OF HISTORY

Modern Literature makes a distinction between myths and mythology. In Ancient Indian Literature no such distinction was observed. For example, in the introduction, the epic Mahabharata is described alternately as Itihasa, Purana and Akhyana. Sometimes, Itihasa-Purana is called the Fifth Veda, as in the Arthashastra. Veda usually means sacred learning or sacred texts, but it may also be construed to signify scientific lore then understood, e.g. Ayurveda, the science of Medicine, Gandharvaveda, that of Music. The English equivalent of Itihasa is History, of Purana Mythology, and of Akhyana legend or story. In addition, we have the Gathas or cycles of folk-tales usually sung by the bards. This welter of terms has created confusion in the mind of many historians, made them remark unfavourably on the nature and continuity of Indian History, and led them to harp on the absence of any historical sense among Indians. Obviously, the sociological significance of the evolution of rituals, myths and mythologies in the unrecorded but the most formative period of History has not yet been seized by the historians of India we read.

Mythology represents a stage of social development later than what is pictured by myths. Myths do, of course, persist and get mixed up with mythology. But it is in the nature of all change to carry over vestiges of the past. The mythological stage is chiefly occupied by semi-divine beings, mostly princes and warriors, and the action is of glorious deeds and mighty combats. Not that the common men are out of the picture—in fact they are very much in it, but usually, they are its framework, as vassals, or as worshippers of the divinity in their heroes. Similarly, the story is not always of wars ; it includes the superior exploits of consolidation and pacification before and after the wars. Think of the magnificent Yagnas performed by the puranic kings and the epic heroes, ceremonies which are attended by feudatory chieftains with their mighty hordes and by priests and scholars with their disciples and by the subjects who come from distant regions. The heroes distribute largess to all and sundry, and introduce what may be called 'reforms' on such occasions. Accounts like what we find in the Ramayana and the Mahabharata, or in the various puranas are not at all peculiar to India ; they are to be found in Greek, Roman, German and Norse mythologies. In short, they are the common features of some well-marked period in the history of all peoples, most of whom chose later to record their history on the basis of their conscious memory.

Before we pass on to the next social feature of this age we would like to mention one aspect of these warrior-heroes. Some of them at least are definitely culture-heroes. Usually, they are twin, or they work in two. They are separated later on, but they must seek to unite. At birth, they are commonly exposed and nursed by animals, nymphs, or shepherds. Between birth and the second coming their life is full of hazards, either self-chosen or created by the powers that be who are the usurpers. These heroes, be it noted, are usually artificers, or harbingers of new occupations by the skill in which they defeat their enemies. And when the heroes come to their own after a period of banishment, there is rejoicing and anointment. Numerous instances tumble into our mind. Krishna and Balarama form a pair. Krishna's life is jeopardized by Kansa, but it is saved by the cowherds. Shakuntala is exposed by her mother (like Semiramis, the legendary queen of Assyria) and she is reared by the birds and the hermit Kanva. For Rome, we have Romulus and Remus suckled by the wolf; for ancient Iran, there is the story of King Cyrus exposed to danger at birth and reared by the shepherds again. In maritime countries, the culture-heroes sail out in boats and canoes. In the Beowulf, Scyld is set adrift on a ship. But all of them return. Probably, the most popular story of the second coming is that of King Arthur. And may we point out here how the hope of the hero's return survives in modern times? The aborigines of the Hawaii islands killed Captain Cook, but they are still expecting that he will come back.

All this similarity must mean something, and anthropologists have unfolded the meaning. It is this: the mythology of the culture-hero represents a transition from one culture-stage to another. He is the mediator or the creator of the novel features of the next phase. No longer is creation in the hands of forces of nature, sun, moon, and the stars, plants and animals; it is now the work of human agency. But the human is quasi-divine; note the stories of birth of the heroes; they are either divinely or immaculately conceived. Still the human element dominates, because in the evolution of society the hero is the great transformer.

Which leads us to the second important feature of this age. It is an age in which the ancient ethic is changed. That ethic was principally based upon the kingly duties and demands, centering in kingly sacrifices. Economically, that ethic was concerned more with the gifts of nature for consumption, now we see the birth of productive technique. Our heroes are artificers, producers, craftsmen, and they win by their craft and skill in carpentry, pottery, fire-making, and the like. Sociologically, this period registers a sort of popular upheaval against the usurpers. The shepherds and cowherds are outside the pale of those who rule. They are the pastoral people tending their flock in the woods and open spaces. They rear the heroes. Combine these economic and sociological features, and you get a glimpse into the beginnings of history, the factors which changed it.

So long we have been talking about early mythologies. Mythologies too have their evolutions and rhythms. The Ramayana is older than the Mahabharata ; both are earlier than the Jataka legends ; and the eighteen Puranas follow them with Upapuranas and Akhyanas, Mahatamyas and Upakhyanas. But this is not to be taken as a chronological sequence. If we go by the nuclei of the stories, the Mahabharata seems to be older than the Ramayana, although the latter as a whole seems to have been known to the makers of the Mahabharata. The core of some of the Puranas also goes back to the Vedas, though we hear of a Purana in which Queen Victoria's name is mentioned ! In any case, there is a sequence which is social, economical and political, that is to say, historical in all sense but the merely chronological. Even in chronology, at least one scholar thinks that the Puranic dates are plausible, provided the knowledge of their measure is known.

Is there any doubt about the fact that the Ramayana tells us a story of the Aryan infiltration into the South of the Vindhyas, and the Mahabharata another story of the supreme attempt of the Aryans to establish the hegemony of one dynasty over tribal chieftains ? The Ramayana is essentially a history of expansion, the Mahabharata, one of consolidation. Naturally, the social context, the system of political alliances, the courtly rules, the laws of administration and warfare are different in these two epics. Similarly, differences are there between the Iliad and the Odyssey, and the various strands of the Norwegian sagas and the German Niebelungenlied. In India, the Puranas proper, as a whole, conjure up visions of a country which had long been stabilized in almost every sphere.

What exactly do we find in these eighteen Puranas ? They have five *lakshanas*, or characteristics. The first is the story of creation, the second is one of re-creation, i.e. the periodic *pralaya* or annihilation and *sristi* or creation. Then we have accounts of succession of gods and sages followed by those of *manvantar* or crisis at the end of which the human race begins again with a new ancestor. And lastly, we get the *Vamsacharita* or the history of dynasties, the Solar and the Lunar in particular. It is this *Vamsacharita* which has helped modern historians so much in the act of re-constructing our past. We can mention here only a few cases of assistance. The historical dynasties of the Sisunagas, Nandas, Mauryas, Sungas, Andhras and Guptas are actually mentioned there. The facts given in the Visnu-purana of the Maurya dynasty (386-185 B.C.) have been proved to be very reliable, as Vincent Smith has said in his *Early History of India*. In the same way, the Matsya-purana gives a true picture of the Andhra dynasty, and the Vayu-purana of the rule of Chandragupta I of the Guptas. 'Scientific' historians have accepted these parts of the Puranas as authentic. Other portions are not so sure in details, but they never fail to offer us the genuine background of those times. For example, the Puranas prophesy the end of a period and say that Kali Yuga had begun. When we know from other sources, e.g. of the Chinese pilgrim, Sung-Yun's and of Kalhana's accounts, that the Huns, Sakas, Tusaras, Gardabhas, Yavanas, Abhiras were flooding the country in this period, we can easily understand how the Aryans became perturbed and pessimistic about the system they had raised in all faith in its permanence. Really, if one reads these Puranas carefully one cannot but notice their value as first-class social records, records of the rise and fall of kingdoms and religious systems, the sects of Vishnu and Siva, of the rights and duties of castes, the life in the forest-asylums and of the various arts and rituals outside. As Dr Winternitz has put it in his encyclopædic *History of Indian Literature* : 'The Puranas are valuable to the historian and to the antiquarian as sources of political history by reason of their genealogies, even though they can only be used with great caution and careful discrimination. At all events they are of inestimable value from the point of view of the history of religion. . . . They afford us far greater insight into all aspects and phases of Hinduism—its mythology, its idol-worship, its theism and pantheism, its love of God, its philosophy and its superstitions, its festivals and ceremonies, its ethics than any other work.' We fully share this great scholar's regret that they have not yet received the attention they deserve. It may be interesting to know, however, that long before the sense of nationalism came to assist the historian of India.

Tagore had pleaded for myths, mythologies and folk-tales as the *basic* materials of Indian History and as the clue to the understanding of its social processes.

In conclusion I should like to emphasize one or two aspects of mythology which may stand our historians in good stead. An eminent thinker, Nicolas Berdyaev, has a pregnant sentence in his book *The Meaning of History*. Says he : 'Mythology is the original source of human history.' For him, the mythological process is the enactment in this natural, terrestrial scene of the drama of human destiny which had its prologue in Heaven. 'It is the second act in eternity but the first in man's terrestrial history.' According to this author, the true meaning of History is the working out of man's destiny in eternity. Well, modern historians may fight shy of eternity and do actually refuse to get lost in its largeness. But, if the task of the historian be to interpret a period in its own spirit and his duty be to desist from importing his own into it, then it is clear that he will have to recognize the altogether different conception of time that pervaded the mythologies. In fact, their units of time, the flow of time, its duration and tempo, were not the same as ours. The time of mythologies had a larger rhythm and a larger interval. If that be so, their implicit philosophy of Time, that is to say, of History, cannot be equated to that of this age. For aught I know, our notion of Time is that it travels in one direction, viz. from the past into the future. Its equivalent philosophy is Progress, of which we have made a secular Religion. On the other hand, in the mythologies, Time is more or less rooted in some timeless past of the golden age since when there has been a regression. Indian mythologies have developed this idea more fully than others. We have our Satya, Treta, Dwapara and Kali Yugas, each followed by a crisis or *manvantar*. But the story is not one of constant regression. At each crisis an Avatar or a Divine Man appears to set matters right. Probably, the concepts of cycles and Avatars will not suit this age and its temper. But, to my mind, the idea of Crisis is very pertinent to this age.

Be that as it may, one thing is beyond dispute: the mythologies in their confusion of facts and fancies do actually represent the attempt of ancient peoples to conquer the flow of time by fixing it in the epic tales of magnificent men and women and their heroic endeavours, and fixing them very surely as symbols in the mind of the common people.* We know how bards chanted the legends and made them remembered by all down the course of ages. These stories are the tokens, the store and the standard of a people's culture. They are, in a very real sense, the first social origins of a people's history. And may I add, the origins sometimes stage a come-back at critical periods in the life of peoples? Man is a myth-making animal, and in the world of mythology he synthesizes dreams with realities and makes of it a 'subject-object world of facts and symbols'. After all dreams, symbols and myths are also data, even if they may not be the primary ones. To find their relation to the primary data, viz. the social operation of living by the common people, in the double process of mutual influence, is an important task for the Indian historian. History may not have occurred or been recorded in India for the sole benefit of research-

*Vide Mrs Langer's *Philosophy in a New Key*. Ch. VII

scholars, but it has been felt and lived up to as a social code by the people. If chronology or archaeology be called the vertical co-ordinate, myths and mythologies form the horizontal one. And you cannot draw a graph or chart with only one—can you?

4. HISTORY AND PERSONALITY

'The significance of historic personalities lies altogether outside of their intrinsic character; their personality serves only as the exponent and the representative; and frequently the distortion between the personality as such and its significance "for others" goes so far that the living individual sees all the importance attached to something which to him mattered least of all.' I came across the above sentence while idly turning over the pages of Count Keyserling's *Das Spektrum Europas* in its English translation entitled *Europe*. This magnificent book I first read in 1929, and since then I often dip into it for the poetic-metaphysical interpretation of human motives and national characters. It does my materialism a lot of good. It often balances my tilt towards History. Sometimes it puts a brake upon the headlong rush of my faith in class-conflict as a major impulse behind social movements. I don't believe in Keyserling's Ethology, but his observations are often very revealing. My copy is full of marginal notes. One such on the quotation at the beginning runs as follows: 'Yes, but did Napoleon become N. to behave like the representative man of the world in the hands of Emerson; or Cromwell a hero to illustrate Carlyle's theory? The tragedy of distortion arises from the difference between content and meaning, between meaning and representative significance, between being and becoming, fact and history.' That was in 1929.

If I were to comment again I would write somewhat like this: 'Not true for Gandhiji for whom intrinsic character is the same as extrinsic, historical character.

The universe of private and public discourse is one and indivisible for him. Neither true for Lenin, vide Anna Krupskaya's Memoirs and Edmund Wilson's *To the Finland Station,* chapters on Lenin. Partly correct for Jawaharlal whose intrinsic personality is aesthetic, in my view. Jinnah is predominantly the representative type. No abandon to emotionality integrates his two personalities. Wonder if he is trying to forget something which he cherishes. He and Jawaharlal meet, in solitude. How would they behave? Like porcupines who throw quills the more they want to come together? Tragic beings: But movement and crisis select the type, and often integrate. Not always. After achievement, which is only the movement in suspense, heroes become symbolic; before crisis, they are often common, very common, vide Marat of France. In literature cf. Gamelin, in A. France's *Gods are Athirst,* a prig who thought that "the French Revolution was an outburst of his righteousness"; also Tikhon of *War and Peace,* whose symbolism is Tolstoy's own—peasantism. In Indian epics, we have heroes; in modern Indian literature none but the romantic editions of historical personalities and the eponymous ones. Read opening para of *The Eighteenth Brumaire.*'

Marginal comments are necessarily brief, but the subject branches out luxuriantly. Keyserling's sentence raises the problem of integration of personality and its place in History. I have often thought that a man who is alleged to have made history has an inner incompatibility between his constituent elements. Such instability generates a force that would explode and burst hard bonds. It seizes the man and makes him do its bidding. It is direct, ruthless, and overwhelming. No wonder that it will be called daemon, genius, *deva, ishta-devata.* After other parts of the man are subjugated, it would loom large like the Frankenstein monster. But, probably, the surrender would not be total and permanent. The subjected elements would raise their head in the shape of passion, foible, or common homeliness. Julius Cæsar must have his Cleopatra, Napoleon must write love-letters to his Josephine or cheat at cards, and Frederick and Karl Marx compose poems or quarrel with friends. The sand beneath the oyster-skin, some canker, some ancient guilt, some unequal tempo in growth, some inner conflict, I once considered to be the sole source of historical greatness and the main reason for the distortion of personality and its twin significance.

Tolstoy, however, would contradict my theory. He paints Napoleon as the wavering, insignificant little corporal, another tennis-ball of Fortune, a mere plaything in the hands of gigantic forces released by the small efforts of millions of common men. Tolstoy pleads for the sanity of the humdrum. It is an amiable doctrine for one like me, a common man doing his drudgery and calling it culture to keep his self-respect by inflation. It heavily discounts the draft 'great' men overdraw on the patience of ordinary folk. It scores the Chinese proverb, 'Great men are public misfortunes'. It fact, it rationalizes our sense of inferiority and uplifts it into a theory of history. It even moralizes envy by abolishing natural differences which now appear as tricks of luck or publicity. But even Tolstoy's own life belies his theory. If ever there was a man built physically, intellectually, morally and spiritually on large and spacious proportions, it was he. He played the primitive Christian, yet he was the sophisticated *barin*, Count Leo

Tolstoy, to his finger tips. He would play the saint, but he was inordinately lustful. He dismissed Art as Art, but he is one of the greatest artists the world has produced. It is not a kink that one notices in his make-up, it is a whole chasm that divides him. Read Leon, Birukoff, Maude, Sarolea's biographies, Gorki's most penetrating estimate, the diaries of the wife and the reminiscences of the daughter, and you realize that this oceanic man nursed two continents in his soul, the European and the Asiatic. The primitive natural paganism of boundless steppes that rolled out into space and Byzantium's orthodox asceticism that reached out to the other world were, to change the metaphor, the two horizon-seeking co-ordinates that intersected in this native Russian product. The uncommon man trying to be a common man is nearly as pathetic as a common man posing as the uncommon. In one case, it is pity, in the other, it is pride. Tolstoy's humility was spiritual pride inverted. No, I cannot accept this divided individual's world-view or his view of man's destiny. The value of both is compensatory, not organically sincere.

What, after all, is the case for the common man? That he has a bond, a 'religion' in the philological sense, a *dharma,* which means the same thing, that which holds together; that he is well-adjusted to his place, folk and time. But is adaptation the be-all and the end-all? Will not man react to the changing world? Is there no such thing as a dynamic equilibrium distinct from the static? Surely, adaptation is not of one variety, viz. the passive. There has always been active adaptation. Again, the process of adaptation is not of a uniform, homogeneous quality; on one level, it is of the worm to the intestines, the fungus to the bark, the peasant to the soil, the savage to his tribal traditions, and the common man to the given ; on another and higher level, the organism gives and takes, and the greater the complexity of the interaction, the more active becomes the role of the organism. With the emergence of civilized man Nature herself yields to his importunate demands. More and yet more links join man with Nature. Geography no longer remains physical, it becomes human. Modern man upsets the original symbiosis, turns the balance of the flora and the fauna, and seeks an optimum on a different layer of existence. Think of the dust-bowl of the States and of the way in which the river-system of the Gangetic delta has been disturbed by the railways : Think of deforestation, floods and soil-erosion : Think of the rubber plantations in Java and Malaya and the changes they have brought in the pattern of life in those countries. The restless spirit of man will not allow him to remain common. Commonness of man is a myth. It is the old individualism in a new garb. No individual as such ever existed. He was created to suit a particular situation in which machines could not but reduce human beings into discrete atoms. He was manufactured to secure his labour-power. He was used to cover exploitation. Once, this individual was called a man of character, a successful man, a go-getter. Now that the days of competition demanding the virtue of ruthless vigour, called self-help, are over, the individual is being re-baptized as the Common Man, i.e. as one who should always remain quiet, loyal, ever yours obediently. The century of the Common Man is no new century ; it is the carry-over of the nineteenth. Wallace's Social Philosophy is only the philosophy of the Open Shop at home, and Open Door in China. It is the cult of the old pioneering type coming home like a chastened prodigal now that the Wild West is no more, the Trade Unions are becoming mischievously strong, and surplus is accumulating for export and investment under the haunting fear of loss of profit. I wish I could call it a plea for stability after all that had happened since 1914. But I cannot, because I am not quite sure about the quality of that stability, and because I know that certain forces making for instability, like the race-question, India's and Africa's problems, have historical justice on their side and will not be appeased unless they are resolved. The cult of the Common Man is a herring across the track of social development. Even if these arguments are found unsatisfactory, how can one forget that Hitler was a very common house-painter and that Mussolini was a common school teacher only the other day? Playing with 'commonness' is a risky affair. Common Man can only mean the exploited being—but that posits a different philosophy of History, a philosophy which is not that of the American Federation of Labour, a body of Common Men one of whom in his representative capacity of commonness has refused to sit at the same table with members of the Russian delegation to the World Trade Union Conference and stood up for the common man's 'free enterprise'.

So I reject the Theory of the Explosive Hero and the theory of the Common Man alike. The geology of the former has faults; the zoology of the latter is parasitical. And yet, the supreme question of integration remains. It must be answered. But how? The Hindus have thrown up the ideal type of the Brahmin, the

Yogi, the Jeeban-mukta, etc.; the Buddhists the Arhat; the Jainas the Jina, the Muni; the early Christians the Saint; the Renaissance the Humanist. Each culture in each epoch has had its own. But the principles of integration have not been contradictory, whatever differences there may have been in shades. Man's place and destiny on earth being held subsidiary to his place and destiny in the other world, his life's functions were so long subordinated to the overriding function of serving the spirit. This simple hierarchy co-ordinated human activities quite effectively. The technique was the law of Karma, faith in the cycle of births and deaths and in transmigration of souls, faith in Grace, God or in supernatural power, Destiny, and the like. But the technique worked only when life's habits and wants were simple, earthly hopes limited to the horizon of the village-common and happiness obtainable inside the paternal acres or the manorial strips. Co-ordination was possible if each man, woman, group, caste was assigned a *swadharma*, and it was done. The social integration of the pre-industrial age was achieved by the Church and the priests in collaboration with the landlord. With the decay of the latter's influence, the priests remained hanging in the air. Man was set adrift, and he floated towards the factories to become an individual unit, carded and numbered. If left to himself he could probably survive the rupture from divinity. But it was not to be. Profit-searching became the ruling passion; it was pursued with the same zeal as the saint had followed his inner light to the gates of Heaven; the owners of machines began to exploit those who tended them; the sense of social organism implicit in the process of production was lost; and with it, the efficiency of the old principles of integration decayed.

It is meaningless to bemoan the glory of lost days, as the neo-Catholic writers seem to be doing with pathetic dignity. Gilson, Maritain, Berdyaev, Neibhur, Eliot, and many more men of genius and learning would want to steer back the arc to some islands of faith. Where are these islands? Do they have ports big enough to hold large ships laden with such heavy cargoes? I am not sure. What then is the alternative? I am not big enough to supply it. But certain conditions for integration suited to the age-emergent may be laid down. The very first condition is to dismiss this idea of the individual and substitute for it that of the person. Personality posits a relation which is not the *versus* relation. Its prepositions are *in*, *through*, and *out*. In other words, personality emerges out by working in and through the given environment. While it is working in, the given is changed. Working through presupposes some conscious direction. With the Kingdom of Heaven out of sight, conscious direction can come only from an understanding of the laws of natural, social, and human development in broad sweeps of stages and tendencies. That is to say, today, History alone can direct. But here is a danger which B. Croce has pointed out. If History, with a capital H, takes the place of some ancient God, then it may easily demand human sacrifices. Quite right. But why should History be a Moloch? I thought Historical Materialism meant the *making* of History and not the destruction of Man. And I know that while some History has been made in the country which is committed to Historical Materialism, while a certain interpretation of its working has been given and held to be sacrosanct for each stage of that country's development, the process of History-making is not yet ended there. In truth, the process is being vigorously pursued today, at this hour, in fields, factories, battle-fields and in high councils. Historical Materialism does not block social movement as the cult of the Common Man is likely to do. It does offer a sense of social direction ; it can partially integrate thereby the modern man, and place him on the way to be a person.

Partially still, not fully, because the problem of emerging out survives. Some think that that's the whole problem. Strictly speaking, however, it is not even the ultimate problem. It is only an attendant problem of later stages. If the word 'problem' is to be used at all in this connexion, it must mean a different need of the adjustment of novel, emergent functions on a higher level. At this stage, one can at best predicate the need of the next, but not that of some remote stage. The task of envisaging some distant future is a luxury which anybody who believes that values are primarily, but not wholly, relative to the age can ill-afford. Vision is the poet's function, and Historical Materialism, if anything, is neither poetic nor prophetic. Its attitude is scientific in the sense that it is cautious to commit itself to prophecy, while retaining the urge for absolute certainty. It does not say that the absolute certitude can be or cannot be known. It only asks for active co-operation with the tendencies towards it. In that historically conscious action lies freedom. It has been wrongly alleged that in Historical Materialism theory is finally and always tested by action. That interpretation suffers from all the defects of Empiricism and Instrumentalism. None of the masters of Historical Materialism understood it in that way, so far as I know. How could they when they knew that the general development of society, its material foundation, the skeleton structure of its organization bore no direct relation to Art in the golden ages, that production was not identical even with legal relationship, that the subtler the ideas, the remoter the connexion, the more tenuous the correlation. At the extreme end one can always feel that the link is broken and the reflection is not there. Historical Materialism only points out that the reflection is still to be seen if only the mercury-coating behind the mirror were there. It further asserts that the blurred image is neither an independent entity nor a prior impulse. It warns men that integration is not possible with the help of images; it suggests that integration is feasible in this world and in this age by an understanding of the laws of social relations and actively co-operating with them. But the world is not ended, and I am not H. G. Wells.

5. THE SENSE OF HISTORY

No, no, there is something rotten in the temple of Clio. Once she was worshipped with the incense of nationalism, now she is being wooed by the pickaxe and the shovel of archaeology. Inscriptions are plastered all over and monuments raised all round her abode, until a scientific treatise on Indian history looks like an American billionaire's castle in his estate, a mass of ruins meticulously arranged to display the taste of wealth. Such a treatise is alleged to be written with a reverence for the 'scientific attitude'. Very often, however, a sense for facts, or a conscience for conclusions, betrays an incapacity for seizing the values; the historian's conscience is just good for making a coward of him, and the regard for 'scientific attitude' becomes a rationalization of having missed the process. If scientific history is not instinct with the sense of history, it is not worth reading by anybody but the poor student preparing for the examination. I think, such books should have limited editions only. The fact of the matter is this: Inscriptions, monuments, records, etc. are the dead ends of a particular strand of the historical process. They are not the materials of history, just as squirrels and bats and birds are not the materials of the history of aeroplanes. Inscriptions etc. have had their history, but they are not history,—of which the main content is the living process and the chief purpose is to re-make it by the study of its laws. Any account that builds on such 'materials' can only lead to generalizations which cover the 'bad conscience and the evil intent of apologetic' to parade as the pursuit of truth.

What exactly is meant by the sense of history? Let me first state what it is definitely not. Its movement is not the chance collocation of individual wills; nor is it the sport of accidents. It is not irrational. Any sequence which it posits is not a march towards a far-off divine event. Nor is it an idea of the ideas that make history. On the other hand, it is also not a monistic explanation as of Feurbach who so eloquently pleaded for beans for bringing about a revolution in Ireland the blood of which being potato-blood was inadequate for the purpose. Exactly on this ground, the sense of history discards transcendental explanation in terms of the spirit or of the race, of the British hypocrisy or Mr Jinnah's 'cussedness'.

The sense of history is rational. It seizes the essentials of people's behaviours, their interactions and their continuities. It is an understanding of the laws of change. It is grounded on the conviction that Man is Nature, that Man remakes Nature, that the difference between Man and Nature is not such as to warrant the abjuration of that method which has succeeded so well in discovering and thus understanding Nature's laws and thereby in partly remaking Nature. Therefore, the sense of history is creative understanding, and consequently understandingly creative. Understanding is neither the cunning of the detective nor the intelligence of a trained advocate. It is also not the intuition of the women's 'I told you so'. It is shrewdness, cleverness, intelligence, all combined, and yet something more. I would add 'intuition', only if that word meant the *dynamics* of ratiocination. Understanding is still not exhausted. Its emergent quality comes from being possessed by what Whitehead would call historical reason, by the laws of process and change, in short, by the laws of Dialectics. A panoramic succession, as seen by Pickwick from the top of the mail-coach, or a cyclical view contemplated by Hegel from the Potsdam terrace, is not the historical process. In the case of Pickwick, it is too discontinuous to yield a regularity ; in the case of Hegel, it is too closed, however big the sweep, to permit the freedom of human making. A sense of history lost in the serial succession is sensational history whereas that which is imprisoned by an irrefragable necessity is history made to order, a command-performance of the Absolute.

One point has to be made clear : it is the connexion between the sense of history and the role of personality or leadership.* There are at least two ways of looking at it, Carlyle's and Tolstoy's. The first seeks to interpret history as a series of biographies of great men or Heroes, and the second dismisses individuals as little corporals, mere playthings of chance or blind forces. It is the former view which is the more dangerous of the two today, in India, where Mahatmaji is held to have moulded Indian history and Mr Jinnah created a whole nation. At least one authoritative book proclaims that the history of India since 1920 is the biography of Mahatmaji. My whole soul likes to believe it, but the sense of history as I have defined it understands the part played by Mahatmaji in the history of India to be as important as the part played by Indian history in the life of Mahatmaji. If the Indian social forces had not

* S. Hook's *The Hero in History* came to the author's hands rather late. Although interesting, it is not penetrating. Plekhanov's treatment of the rôle of the individual still remains the best.

selected him to represent them he would not have been effective in moulding them and strengthening them. It is not a matter of a mechanical give and take ; it is dialectical. At times Mahatmaji has been rejected by India ; he has waited, and India's level of vigilance has gone low ; he has again come back when India has selected him, and the level has once again gone up. But it will be long before Mahatmaji gets his historical meed of praise in the Oxford, Cambridge, or the future London Imperial (Commonwealth) history of India. After that Indian 'scientifics' will not touch him. The same fate awaits Mr Jinnah and Pandit Jawaharlal Nehru. But the immediate danger is from the chauvinist. Be that as it may, a historian with the sense of history puts the leader in the perspective of critical changes, shows how he seizes the revolutionary moment in the objective situation, clarifies the issues involved, and in the process of clarification, unfolds how he furthers the cause of change in the socially desired direction with the help of the latent drives in the developing situation. Beyond this signification the sense of history becomes romantic and transcendental, which is only the other side of the mechanistic view. I wonder if the scientific attitude of the Indian scientific historians betrays any symptom of the proper historical sense in their treatment of men like Asoka or Akbar. In the descriptions of the contemporary social and political conditions as given by our scholars one searches in vain for the revolutionary situation which Asoka or Akbar or Shivaji pounced upon like an eagle. Nor is there much of an account of the issues which they clarified or precipitated. And yet, nothing else can explain the greatness of these individuals.

What the scientific attitude in History has given to Indian History is accuracy. But this accuracy belongs to that low order where facts remain facts. Inasmuch as the sense of History deals with events, and not with the facts *per se*, it is only intellectual honesty to enquire into the reasons why facts have not yet been understood and 'converted' into events by Indian historians. I submit that the academic reason is not in the inability, but in the method practised. The scientific method followed is of the nineteenth century, if not of an earlier age. Recent advances in logic have shaken certain parts of the foundations of that method and enriched other parts in various ways. Today, we cannot afford to remain content with the accuracy of observation. That is the barest minimum. But more remains to be done. I seriously suggest the writing of a history of the Indian people, not exactly on the model of Green of hallowed memory, but on the lines laid down recently by men of lesser renown, Young on Victorian England, Morton on England, Oliver on Germany, L. Huberman on the U.S.A., to take only a few examples. The flag of science will not be lowered ; it will rally the indifferent and the down-hearted.

6. 'HISTORY MAY BE SERVITUDE, HISTORY MAY BE FREEDOM'

Some of the best defence of the traditional values of European culture has come from the Americans. While Europe chooses to remain cultured, a number of American writers have devoted themselves to the task of explaining what European culture is. There was a time when the Americans felt nostalgic about their 'home-land' and sighed for its values. But a reaction set in, and the 'pioneering literature' was discovered. It was felt that in the cauldron of peoples that was the U.S.A. new contents were brewing and new shapes were emerging, that if the contents had not the status of those which on the other side of the Atlantic gave the stock literary responses, if they were too crude and immature, their novelty and raw humanity, their vigour and urge to live were sufficient compensations. And the feeling was not just a manifestation of any anti-European or a mere patriotic attitude. It might have been partly that with a few authors, but its essence was generally different. No sentiment that springs in opposition can account for the genuineness of Bret Harte's stories of the camps, Mark Twain's Huckleberry Finn, or Whitman's free verses. Nor is patriotism a key to the strength of modern novelists like Dreiser, Faulkner, or Dos Passos. The true reason is that for the U.S.A., history had once been servitude, but now it is freedom.

Mr T. S. Eliot's position is slightly different. To apply Gerald Heard's apt phrase, he is a 'Time-haunted man' who wants to develop a 'Time-understanding mind'. He will shed his affiliations to Time, and therefore, to Place as well, through Christianity. In 'Little Gidding', a remarkable poem, he seeks liberation from the future as well as from the past. For him

> 'The moment of the rose and the moment of the
> yew-tree
> Are of equal duration. A people without history
> Is not redeemed from time, for history is a pattern
> Of timeless moments!'

If we leave its metaphysic (Buddhist Kshanikavada ?) to the learned and take up the cultural aspect only, we at once see, in the next line, how for Mr Eliot the servitude of American history has flowered into the freedom of English history.

> 'So, while the light fails
> On a winter's afternoon, in a secluded chapel
> History is now and England.'

Mr Eliot, the American's redemption is in the line of Henry James', only his naturalization-papers are adorned with Christian and Buddhist texts. His servitude is over, and for him the freedom of history is of another pattern, not American at any rate, but purely personal, and thoroughly England's.

My concern here is not with the literary qualities of the poem. Mr T. S. Eliot, the poet who makes poems, is very dear to us Indians. We share with him many things in common. We fully endorsed his *Waste Land*, and got some poetry into the bargain. Mr Eliot's metaphysic is so familiarly Anglo-Indian! We too progress from Mr Prufrock to the Yogi seeking liberation, incidentally passing through that indifference which is neither attachment to self, things, or persons, nor detachment from the same, but is just

> 'Being between two lives
> Unflowering, between the live and the dead nettle.'

And here is the doubt. We too want redemption from

the History that is servitude, but shall it be the History that is freedom ? While light fails inside the prison-walls can we really sing with him ' History is now and England ? ' Some do, and they ' write ' our history !

But in what spirit ? Most of us have had to wade through ponderous tomes on Ancient, Medieval, and British India. We profited by them in our examinations. But on turning over their pages once more, if we can persuade ourselves to that task, we have a feeling that the history of India in the hands of her historians has been a story of the regression of human spirit, its diminution and shrinkage. In this matter Indian writers are as guilty as the European writers. The former glorify pre-Muslim India and record the subsequent deterioration ; the latter may or may not be eloquent over the first but agree about the second with a view to praising Pax Britannica. Barring Akbar's reign, there is a black-out submerging the glorious Renaissance of the so-called Middle Ages, their synthesis of cultures, their philosophies, their æsthetics, and their social experiments. Anybody who is not blinded by prejudice against the Muslims or for the British cannot but conclude, on the basis of reliable evidence to be had in sources other than the familiar ones, that once more in the course of her history India was being made in that period. The reason for silence on that matter cannot be the absence of materials. It is the wrong approach towards History, the wrong way of writing it. And the supreme pity is that it has been all in the name of science, that science which in its entanglements with the mechanical view-point in philosophy neglected the freedom of collective human willing and action and had to strangle the past by the dead-weight of chains.

The fact of the matter is this : Our historians have not faced the past in their eagerness to keep its face. 'The past must be faced, or,' as Benedette Croce puts it in his *History As The Story of Liberty*, 'not to speak in metaphors, it must be reduced to a mental problem which can find its solution in a proposition of truth, the ideal premise for our new activity and our new life. This is how we daily behave, when instead of being prostrated by the vexations which beset us, and of bewailing and being ashamed by errors we have committed, we examine what has happened, analyse its origin, follow its history, and with an informed conscience and under an intimate inspiration, we outline what ought and should be undertaken and willingly and brightly get ready to undertake it. Humanity always behaves in the same way when faced with its great and varied vast. The writing of histories—as Goethe once noted—is one way of getting rid of the weight of the past. Historical thought transforms it into its own material and transfigures it into its object, and the writing of history liberates us from history.'

Will our historians who have undertaken to write our history—they are all idealists who cannot object to Croce—'outline what ought and should be undertaken' so that the young readers may 'willingly and brightly get ready to undertake it'? Our experience has been unfortunate. Let the future citizens not have it again. They have every right to expect that the new writing will at least liberate them from history. For us History has been servitude, in the name of 'science'; for them let History be freedom, for the sake of making it. We have been betrayed; shall we betray the future generation by robbing their History of its Freedom?

7. DEMANDS ON THE INDIAN HISTORIAN

No Indian reader who is interested in the future of India will be placated by any future volume or volumes on her history unless the following conditions are fully or partly satisfied therein. The fact that they have not been fulfilled so far only sharpens the edge of the urgency. Be it noted that the demand is not prompted by any mere romantic attachment to the geographical entity of India but by a faith in India's destiny measured by the positive balance of successes and failures in her peoples' favour. Her past is not a glorious march from progress to progress, nor is it an unbroken series of failures. But the sum-total has a momentum which keeps the Indian still going, retaining an integrity that has fallen apart in more dramatic and triumphant cultures. The common man of India, illiterate, poor, exploited as he is, is still a whole man. He has a store of values from which he draws a code of conduct which is still aristocratic, if not in its gift of leadership, at least, certainly, in the stoic unruffledness of organic sensibility and behaviour. In China too the common man is the inheritor of similar legacies ; which only means that similar conditions may be demanded by the average Chinese in the writing of Chinese history. In fact, it is this *integrity* of the common man in the midst of disruption which makes the Chinese and the Indian cultures so akin. And modern Chinese historians seem to be well aware of this solar centrality of their scholarship. Be that as it may, there must be some reason in Indian History to account for the wholeness of the common man of India in spite of the dirt and squalor of his living.

In no sense is this a plea for more poverty ; nor is it a glorification of the common man either of American publicists and statesmen or of Indian romantics ; it is only a cardinal fact about the submerged Indian. After all, Indian History is a story of her peoples, and, in the last analysis, peoples mean individuals. If statements by leaders of the United Nations speak of the post-war era as that of the Common Man, then Indian History rightly written may also tell the world about the procedure by which the common man in India has been saved from the vulgarity that attends poverty and exploitation. Thus the first condition of the writing of Indian history by Indian historians is revealed. It is an explanatory account of the persistence of the wholeness of the common man in India in spite of vicissitudes. In other words, Indian History must needs be the history of Indian culture—not, the course of politics but the culture-pattern which has held so far. Evidently, it is also the social pattern into which Indian culture has been woven. A textbook which relegates the growth of rituals and symbols, of philosophy and literature, to a concluding chapter or of music to a footnote, which ignores the declining status of women or of the untouchables, which omits to mention the changes in the caste-system or in the relation between village-life and urban-life, which fails to show the impact of a new faith upon the life of the people—that textbook does not explain India to her people or to the world. Call it anything, but the Indian historian must seize the philosophy of it all. His method cannot but be systematic, rigorous and disciplined, but he will have to preface it by understanding the staying capacity of the common man in the Indian field and workshop. A corollary to the above is the recognition, and then the explanation, of the fact that the 'uncommon' men of India, the so-called 'middle-classes', of the professions, in business and in services are men of straw, hollow men, pseudo-human. Lest there be a misunderstanding, let me repeat: the recognition of the historical fact of the common man of India's integral persistence is *not* a plea for competitive individualism, *not* a praise of its values, *not* a plaint to allow it to function as such. The common man in India does *not* mean the petty *bourgeois*.

The next condition is the 'sociological' approach. As there is much loose thinking about the term, a few words are needed to explain it. A mention, even a detailed one at that, of the social background of a given political situation is not Sociology. Sociology is the study of group-behaviours and their inter-relations. Therefore, it is more comprehensive than the sum-total of a number of disciplines. It has its own scope which is not residual but which cuts across the scopes of other sciences, like Economics, Jurisprudence, Politics, Ethics. That scope is of the whole pattern and process of human group-behaviour. That obstinate, stubborn, persistent core which subsumes the changes is the starting point of Sociology. History rings the changes and Sociology offers the unity and the continuity. They are the Purusha and the Prakriti of the social sciences. Once the start from the unity and continuity of the social process is made, History assumes a different form. Then the Pathan and the Mughal rules do not appear to be foreign or non-Indian, but phases in Indian History, giving a shock to one strand of the basic pattern or strengthening another, and energizing the whole process by diverse means. Then the character of the 'British period' unfolds itself as a revolutionary one with the impact of Western capitalism upon India's feudal division of labour, family-organization and caste. Then also is the capital lesson of History learnt—that it proceeds by spurts and jumps, while it is only preserved by a peaceful evolutionary continuance. India too, as only the sociologist can tell, has had to face catastrophic changes, and she has transmuted them into agencies for survival. If the technique of the transmutation has not helped her to form a dynamic State, as the world today understands it, if it has failed to make the spirit plunge into the material to create healthy conditions of living for the common people, then the explanation will not lie with the 'scientific' or the 'pure' historian busy with dates and monuments, scripts and colophons, but it will rest with the historian who is instinct with Sociology. In other words, Sociology must inform History. Elsewhere it has done so. Not History alone, it has impregnated Science itself. Even in conservative England where Sociology leads an apologetic existence, the British Association have been compelled to discuss in their annual sittings the social implications of Science. Literary criticism has been deeply influenced by it. And so have Economics and Jurisprudence. Only the historians of India stand aloof. When we remember that India has had more of society than of the State, that her religions have penetrated into the inmost recesses of living, that Hinduism is more of a culture than of a religion or a philosophy in the European sense, that Buddhism, Jainism, Islam, Sikhism and other religions have survived more by diffusion than by political prestige, then this absence of the sociological approach is not only a criminal conduct but a blunder of the first magnitude. If there are Indian heads broken in communal riots today, well, a great deal of the responsibility lies on the head of the 'pure' historian of India. Our history is pre-eminently a social process. To miss the sociological approach is to keep India servile by serving Indians with 'pure' but partial History. Ignorance can be excused, but rationalization of ignorance in the name of 'science' never. It has proved too costly. We simply cannot afford it.

8. HISTORY AS CONTEMPLATION

Jakob Burckhardt is one of Europe's great historians. The civilization of the Renaissance in Italy, the only book of his we could get in English translation in our college days, set an almost unattainable standard of historical writing in the depth of knowledge, the sweep of vision and the excitement of adventure. One could occasionally dip into its pages and trace the track of the individual out of the jungle of medieval restrictions, the march of pageantry, and the tortuous evolution of statecraft. If one chose, one could peep into the private lives of dukes, duchesses, popes and courtesans, into the library of encyclopædic men and the galleries of patrons of art. In another mood, one could contemplate the good and the evil of Humanism, of the emergence of the Western man and the decay of religion in that adolescent period of European history. The masterpieces of Italian Art, pictures, statues, architecture, crafts were all there to stimulate the love of beauty which lay crushed in the bosom of every young Indian by the mechanical system of education he had received. So the Phaidon Press conferred a boon on all students of civilization when it republished Burckhardt's treatise in a sumptuous volume, and very recently, in a comparatively cheap edition. Last year, another volume of Burckhardt came out in English under the title *Reflections on History*. It is a very important work, although it is nothing more than a series of rough drafts and notes of lectures he delivered at the University and the Museum at Basle. The professor was so intensively devoted to his University that he once wrote : 'In my very dubious estimate of earthly bliss I find one great lacuna, one exception, and that is this—I regard the existence of the University of Basle not only as desirable in the mundane sense, but as a metaphysical necessity.' The cantons of Switzerland generate a loyalty denied to cosmopolis ; the city of Erasmus and Holbein is also a worthy object of devotion ; but it may be questioned how many Indian scholars could say that about their own Universities or reject the offer of a professorship with higher scale and status as Burckhardt did when he was offered by the mighty Kaiser the post of Ranke at Berlin. And yet, such an attitude was nothing unusual in India. Who again, is the Indian professor today who can be so learned in his public addresses and class-lectures as Burckhardt shows himself to be in these scrappy notes of his ? And where is the public or the student-community in India today who can feel at home in that expanse ? Professors and students, lecturers and audience pull each other down to the level of dull, barren, arid mediocrity. The present intellectual decline in our country has been caused by many outside factors ; but the ever-willingness of scholars to stoop to conquer is certainly one of the inside ones. The *Reflections on History* has occasioned these sad thoughts. We are, however, concerned here with Burckhardt's own reflections which have been described as 'prophetic' by men who should know.

His view of History has been best expressed in his letter to Nietzsche quoted in the introductory note to the volume. 'My poor head was never capable, as yours is, of reflecting upon the ultimate reasons, aims and desirabilities of historical science. Yet as a teacher and lecturer I think I may say that I never taught history for the sake of the thing which goes by the high-falutin name of World History, but essentially as a general subject. . . . I have done what I could to bring them to take personal possession of the past—in any shape or form . . . and at any rate not to sicken them of it. . . . I am well aware that such an aim may be condemned as fostering amateurism, but that does not trouble me overmuch.' Burckhardt was convinced that with the sudden devaluation of the past by the present civilization his duty lay in stressing 'the history of ideas, retaining only an indispensable scaffolding of events'. This procedure, he felt, would not be helpful to academic scholarship, but it would stay, however partially, 'the era of wars' and its dire consequences to which, as Burckhardt saw, Europe was fatally committed. Naive indeed for a citizen of Europe in 1870, but very natural to a professor who had his view of History.

This view was governed by two considerations: 'In particular,' says he, 'we should be able to contemplate the process of history even when it is not concerned with our own well or ill-being, directly or indirectly. But even when it is, we should be able to behold it with detachment.' That such detachment was attained by Jakob Burckhardt in his *magnum opus* is easily admitted. What is not equally admissible is the corollary that detachment offers the complete view. Thus, for example, the rise of Florence, which forms with Rome the two radiating centres of the Renaissance, the birth of the individual, which is the secret of the Renaissance, and the glory that was Italy at the climacteric of the Middle Ages, pass before our eyes in the panoramic succession of pageantry; but the new social forces which weaned away the modern civilization from the medieval are not revealed by Burckhardt with the surety of one whose vision is as complete as it is penetrating. Nobody who owes any account to History will compare him with Huizanga, the author of the *Waning of the Middle Ages,* or Von Martin, the author of *Sociology of the Renaissance,* but for one reader at least, Huizanga is more satisfying on the human and Martin on the material conditions of the Renaissance. The latter's analysis of the new dynamics in terms of the rise and ascendancy of the bourgeoisie is an indispensable complement to Burckhardt's detached beholding.

What sight the historian-contemplator beholds from the 'Archimedean point outside events' is best illustrated in the learned professor's remarks on Islam and Islamic culture. According to Burckhardt, the dynamics of History are supplied by the reciprocal action of three powers, viz. the State, Culture and Religion, in their different permutations. Of these Islam is an instance of the whole of culture being dominated, shaped and coloured by polity which is 'of necessity despotic'. The result of such domination has been described in a number of pages of which 88 and 89 offer the cream. Even if we trace the publication of libellous remarks on a culture and its Holy Book to the fundamental right of expression in freedom-loving England or Switzerland, it is difficult to pardon the gross ignorance of this eminent historian about one of the most important facts of European history, not to speak of the history of a considerable part of Asia and Africa, viz. that the rise and spread of Islam and the Islamic peoples was one of the revolutionary agencies, the vitalizing leaven and a highly effective carrier of cultural change. He would grudge culture even to Muslim Spain and to the age of the Umayyads ! He calls the whole thing a 'fiction'. This opinion, fortunately, is not shared by any historian of consequence. And yet, Burckhardt was a great man. Which can only mean that contemplation at the Archimedean point is no guarantee against prejudice and ignorance. Detachment may often lead to distortion.

The second ruling consideration of Burckhardt's view of History was aversion from 'system' and 'principles'. Says he : 'We shall, further, make no attempt at system, nor lay any claim to historical principles. On the contrary, we shall confine ourselves to observation. . . . Above all, we have nothing to do with the philosophy of history. The philosophy of history is a centaur, a contradiction in terms, for history co-ordinates, and hence is unphilosophical, while philosophy subordinates, and hence is unhistorical.' The reasons for his abjuration of philosophy are two : (a) Philosophy grappling with 'the great riddle of life' 'stands high above history'; and (b) philosophies of history have followed 'in the wake of history', and not come before history ; and so we are not 'privy to the purposes of eternal wisdom' which are beyond our ken. Burckhardt, however, would not mind if the philosophy were 'genuine, that is a philosophy without bias, working by its own methods'. He would also 'not forget the great currents in modern philosophy significant in themselves and throughout associated with historical views'.

The corollary to the above is 'friendship between science and history, not only because, . . . science demands nothing from history, but also because these two branches of learning are alone capable of a detached, disinterested participation in the life of things'. Burckhardt, of course, is fully aware of the fact that the awakening of consciousness effects the breach between nature and history. 'Participation in the life of things', even if it were disinterested, is not contemplation from the Archimedean point. It will be fruitless to point out similar contradictions in the professor's *Reflections*. After all, they were 'reflections' and not integrated into any sustained thesis. Yet, the horror of any philosophy of history is to be noted for its being the ultimate source of the confusion. It is also responsible for the meaningless academic distinction between 'history and the historical'. The real distinction is between the historical and the pre-historical, between history as participation (and the resultant change with the quest for principles as the conscious part) and history as contemplation. There is something seriously wrong with Burckhardt's view of the relation between knowledge and life, i.e. his philosophy, which accounts for his misunderstanding of the functions of history and science. None of these two disciplines has had its origin in contemplation: none can fully satisfy its functions in areas drained of social usefulness; none is allowed by the very urgencies of living to remain detached and disinterested; and none can remain like the Lady of Shallot looking at the mirror, and wait and wait till Crisis come.

And, therefore, Burckhardt's analysis of crisis in history is hardly anything more than a record of events of his own selection. On p.143 the following sentences occur: 'Whether the spirit of an age which paves the way for crisis is the mere sum of many individuals of like mind, or, . . . the higher cause of the ferment, is a question to be left open, like that of liberty or bondage as a whole. In the last resort, the impulse to great periodical changes is rooted in human nature, and whatever degree of average bliss were granted to man, he would one day (indeed, then more than ever) exclaim with Lamartine : "La France s'ennuie." An essential preliminary condition would seem to be a high development of traffic and a widespread similarity of thought on other questions. Yet when the hour and the real cause has come, the infection flashes like an electric spark over hundreds of miles and the most diverse peoples, who, for the rest, hardly know of each other's existence. The message goes through the air, and, in the one thing that counts, all men are suddenly of one mind, even if only in a blind conviction : "Things must change." '

A few comments are necessary. The origin of the spirit of the age paving the way for crisis may be left open, but can its function be so dismissed ? And, 'like liberty or bondage' ! One would much rather subscribe to Croce's view that human history is the history of freedom. Surely, the urge for liberty and hatred of bondage had something to do with the American and the French Revolutions, incidents which had preceded Burckhardt's lectures. We Indians like to feel that the urge of freedom is also rooted in Indian human nature and that the history of the last fifty or sixty years, even if scientifically (not philosophically) written, will be incomplete without the freedom-movement. A further question arises as to why if the impulse to great 'periodical changes' be rooted in human nature it manifests itself in one period and not in another. How to account for the 'periodical changes' in human nature which 'periodical changes' in history involve ? Does man really feel bored with average human bliss and more bored with its increase? If he does, then history becomes French poetry of the last quarter of the nineteenth century, and its contemplation becomes epicurean, and not stoical which one expected from a disciplined mind and character like Burckhardt's. Boredom does not come from bliss; it is Sodom's apple iced and creamed to satisfy the jaded appetite of decadents who must be served on the edge of a volcano. The destiny of ennui for man is an insult to the roots of human nature. And then, 'when' does the 'hour' come? What is the 'real cause'? How does the infection spread? Is 'things must change' a *blind* conviction? If it be conviction, it cannot be blind; if it be blind, it will be faith. We Indians are at least blindly convinced that things must change. Have things changed? If so, is our blind conviction the cause of the changes? The comments may be thus multiplied.

Here comes Philosophy. We will not go into the question of history's having a philosophy or not. But nobody need be a historian if he is not analytical and constructive. In our opinion, philosophy alone can offer the critique of history, the analysis of its forces and the principles of its construction. Burckhardt's view of history as contemplation is flight from life, and so, from the responsibilities of knowledge and crisis. The Indian historian will not profit by *Reflections on History*.

9. ON INDIAN HISTORY

Now that a shape is going to be given to the idea of a comprehensive history of India I beg to submit a layman's point of view for what it is worth. We have had two standard texts on Indian history as a whole and a number of valuable volumes on special periods. Our difficulty with the former has been that we Indians have not been helped by them either to understand the meaning of Indian History and the reasons for its persistence, or to change it and make it anew according to our own light and leanings. The trouble with the latter is that they are too cross-sectional to bear the weight of the traffic, i.e. of the entire process. The man in the street has avoided these difficulties by thinking of Indian History as a jerky series and forgetting all about the continuity and the need for action or making. It works out for him like this : (a) if the Oxford and Cambridge textbooks claim that unity was achieved for the first time under the British Crown, we can posit the counter claim that it had also been secured by the Mauryas, the Guptas, Asoka, Harsha, Akbar and others ; (b) let us string together the researches of K. P. Jaiswal, R. K. Mookerji, Bhandarkar, Sardesai and Sarkar, and a beautiful garland will be made for Bharat-Mata's neck. These two operations coalesce easily in the mind of the common Indian reader who must have some compensation out of life. There is nothing wrong here except that an admiration for the glorious periods is a poor substitute for the study of the ways by which India has been living. The sum total of statuses, however high and glamorous they may be, is not equal in value to the dynamics of History, be they as dull as the Phalgu's current under the sands. We Indians have never been told by the historians that this India is a going concern. Will the new volumes tell us that ?

How very important such a task is will be evident from this typical quotation from a writer who is described and rightly too, as one of the significant thinkers of the century. (It is a pity that Nicolas Berdyaev is not well known in our country.) In one of his later books, *The Meaning of History* (1936), he writes : 'The completely unhistorical or antihistorical nature of the ancient cultures of both India and China is due to the fact that the freedom of the creative subject was not revealed therein. Neither was it revealed in the philosophy of the Vedanta, one of the greatest of the philosophical systems, nor, again, in those philosophies which have a certain conception of freedom as an absolute blend and union of the human and the divine spirits. India, too, ignored the idea of human freedom. And this accounts for the fact that this otherwise original culture lacks an historical character. Thus Christianity was to reveal conclusively the freedom of the creative subject which had been ignored by the pre-Christian world. And this discovery of the inner dynamic principles of history determining the fulfilment of the historical destinies of man, peoples and mankind, eventually produced that eventful world history which coincides with the Christian era'. For our purposes, we should exclude the reference to China and to the Vedanta and keep an open mind to the claim made on behalf of Christianity. Personally, I have no doubt that a very eventful period of universal history opened with the Christian era. I shall go farther and say that European civilization, inclusive of the Soviet civilization, *pace* J. Maritain, is inextricably wound up with the fortunes of the Christian spirit. But a still closer intimacy with N. Berdyaev's views arises from my sympathy with his enunciation of the theme of universal history as that of the person, peoples and mankind's destiny seen in the light of the interaction between human spirit and nature which constitutes the foundation and the motivating principle of the 'historical'. Is there any Indian who will not subscribe to the view that man's historicity ultimately consists in the liberation of the creative human spirit? What else has the Indian nationalist been doing but playing upon that theme these hundred years?

And yet, an Indian historian must, in all humility, take up the challenge that this original culture of India lacks an historical character and prove that the statement is not borne out by the facts about the process of our culture-formation. If he fails here, he remains just a scholar, an archaeologist, discharging the noble but small duties of a labourer in a factory, the wholeness, the direction and the management of which being in other hands are sealed to him in the name of division of labour and technical efficiency. Here is a straight question: Has India a history or not, in Berdyaev's sense? Did India care for human freedom? My information is that India has had cultural history, even if she had not very much of the political or the economic history in the Austinian or the Ricardian sense respectively. I have also been told that this Indian culture has occupied itself with the liberation of the human spirit. If its traditional pre-occupation has been with the obstructions of natural necessity and the ways of surmounting them, then instead of limiting himself to the making of a general statement about the unhistorical or anti-historical character of Indian culture, a historian interested in the meaning of History in general and of Indian History in particular should address himself to the two-fold task of (a) squaring the natural necessity with the social, political and economic necessities which the course of Indian history has collected after the Christian era, specially after the impact of a Christian power, and (b) studying the means for overcoming them in order that the emancipation of the human spirit may be fuller than what it has been so far. In other words, it should be one of the primary duties of our historian to explain why and how our traditional pre-occupation with the conquest of natural necessity and of the baser elements of human nature has changed over into what may be called an obsession with other necessities like those of political freedom, social flexibility and economic betterment. He should also enquire how far this shift in emphasis has been to the good of Indians, and if good, how it can be augmented, if bad, how it can be controlled.

This is quite apart from the possibility that the statement about the un-historical or anti-historical quality of Indian culture is itself an un-historical and anti-historical assertion. As a layman, I posit that Indian culture, being essentially humanistic is one of the grand experiments in unfolding the meaning of Universal History, viz. the freedom of the human spirit and the working out of the destiny of man. From the Vedas, passing through the Muslim period's magnificent synthesis, down to Gandhiji's non-violence, Indian culture has been doing nothing but performing History's own task. India, I feel, is one of the historical units of Mankind. That is my own view. I want to know from our historians if I am correct or not.

But how can they answer me and my like, I mean the average Indian, unless they themselves have a philosophy of history? Or, do they abjure philosophy itself in order to be up to date? Then they are liquidating a first-class Indian asset, viz. India's traditions of philosophy and simultaneously betraying ignorance of modern thinking and practice. Or do they unconsciously separate the historical from History, as Jakob Burckhardt attempted to do in his lectures at Basle, now published as *Reflections on History*? In which case they should be ready to feel happy with the same fallacies, the same misunderstanding. and the same contradictions as Burckhardt committed in course of drawing a fine line between History and the historical. To quote just one instance: (I am doing so to draw the attention of our historians only. and not of our public.) Burckhardt hates Islam and Islamic culture. What is written about them on pp. 87-89 and on p. 136 would have been unprintable in India. But my concern is not with law and order. Those pages betray the confusion implicit in the method itself. The proclaimed exclusion of Philosophy from the study of History (p. 15), the differentiation of the historical from History and the selection of the former as the theme of historical studies (p. 26), the search for the 'Archimedean point outside events' (p. 19), and the advice to 'approach it in a spirit of contemplation' (p. 19), could not but lead that great professor to get entangled in absurdities the like of which no sane person in India would want the Indian historians to commit. Our historians must have a philosophy. If that word stinks, they should have 'a method, a critique'. Otherwise they had better remain professors of History.